The Guide to Effective Supervision

The Guide to Effective Supervision

Richard D. Ollek, CBSE, RGC

authorHOUSE®

AuthorHouse™
1663 Liberty Drive
Bloomington, IN 47403
www.authorhouse.com
Phone: 1 (800) 839-8640

Published by AuthorHouse 06/17/2015

ISBN: 978-1-5049-1743-8 (sc)
ISBN: 978-1-5049-1744-5 (hc)
ISBN: 978-1-5049-1742 1 (e)

Library of Congress Control Number: 2015909465

Print information available on the last page.

CONTENTS

ACKNOWLEDGMENTS

First and foremost I acknowledge our good and gracious God. I give him praise, honor and glory for all the blessings he has provided me throughout my life. His saving grace is available to all who would believe and the knowledge of having him as my guide in all that I do, brings great comfort to me. What a joy.

Next is the important part my wife Barbara has played in my entire life. She married me in 1962 and has been my partner and helpmate in all that I do. Even when I made business decisions that she disagreed with (and I was usually wrong), she was always at my side supporting me during good times and bad. With God and Barbara at my side, life has been a wonderful journey.

My three children who have always been supportive of me even when I wasn't there for all the parenting duties I should have performed-- another credit to their wonderful mother.

And last but not least, my faithful Boston Terrier dog Caesar, who sits by my side as I write books, podcasts, DVD scripts and other material that I hope will help others in their pursuit of improving what they do. What would I do without Caesar? Woof! Woof! Woof! Woof!

All have been so instrumental in whatever I have accomplished in this great life. I am forever thankful and grateful.

DISCLAIMER

Neither the author nor its legal counsel make any representations as to the legality of the ideas or statements contained in this book. They represent the ideas and opinions of the author only, and in no way provide a guarantee of success for the reader, as every company and individual situation will be different as will the commitment to any program or process.

Furthermore, any cost estimates or prices are based on information deemed reliable but not guaranteed and are used for the purpose of illustration only. All persons should consult with their own legal and financial counsel concerning the many questions and issues that may arise. Furthermore, neither the author nor its legal counsel make any claims as to the overall professionalism of any companies mentioned in this book.

WHAT OTHERS ARE SAYING

"Since working with Consultants In Cleaning, LLC, our janitorial customer base grew by 20% within 6 weeks of implementing Dick Ollek's marketing and sales strategies. Our company soon separated itself from the rest in our industry by the professional presentations and sales systems dynamics that we learned. What truly is remarkable and exciting is the residual effects these systems have, even 2 years later we are getting new customers from the original implementation. My favorite part of working with Dick Ollek is that the things I learned from him can be applied in other facets of my business and relationships. Thanks Dick Ollek and Consultants In Cleaning, you truly changed our business AND our lives.

Jennifer L. Bulkley, CSSP, CFO
Advantage Cleaning Systems
Hornell, New York

"A veteran of the building services industry, Dick has seen, said, and done virtually everything you can imagine. As a successful business owner, and now a consultant willing to share with those (like me) who need to learn, Dick "gets it", and when it comes to managing and working with people, I certainly lend a ready ear. In an industry reliant upon human resources to perform and ensure quality work, he's found ways to get the most out of a staff. I look forward to continually working with and learning from Dick and I hope you will too".

Jason Pyne
General Manager
CleanTelligent Software
Provo, Utah

Dick, I love the articles and the information that you provide on LinkedIn. I also look forward to your pod casts and blog posts. It provides me great knowledge about the cleaning industry that we don't have here in Australia.

I credit you with empowering me to become a better manager of my staff and developing a clearer on boarding process for my company.

I can safely say that in the last 2 years I have had a reduction of over 300% in the turnover of my staff. As a result, I have lost no clients because of service issues due to the training and on boarding process I set up after listening to your pod casts and reading your training articles.

So I wish to say thank you for your advice.

Raymond Bowling
Managing Director
Clean Recruits
Australia

INTRODUCTION

While this book can be read like any other book you may buy, it is intended to be used in a different manner than just reading.

It is our desire that you will use it as a teaching tool in your company. You will notice that we have not labeled the sections as chapters but rather as lessons. The idea is that you can use each lesson as a teaching tool for supervisors. Each lesson stands on its own and can be used separately to learn one phase of effective supervision or our suggestion is that you use it as an ongoing learning experience.

We suggest it be used as a once a week session, asking each participant to read the lesson for that week and then have it serve as a lesson plan for discussion the next week.

It is also important that the management of the company interject the policies and procedures of their particular company into each lesson adding or deleting any subject matter from this book as it applies to the individual organization. The lessons are meant only as a guide and reference material to discuss a particular subject in helping an individual become a more effective supervisor.

You may take issue with some of the ideas discussed by the author in these lessons and we encourage that discussion. Each lesson is a guide only and should serve as an outline only.

You will also note as you weave your way through the various sessions that we have repeated some examples in different lessons. This is not because we are forgetful but because we felt that the examples shown or stories relayed had importance in each of the lessons and bore repeating. See if you can recognize or remember the repeats.

At the end of each lesson is a series of questions we pose to the participant and you may wish to add or delete questions as they pertain to your individual company. We welcome that.

If you are an owner or manager of a company, let me suggest you conduct weekly learning sessions with your supervisors and potential supervisors using these lessons. Then print the questions at the end of each lesson and have the participants answer them in writing and hand them back so you can review their comprehension of the material and discuss with them one on one any coaching that may be needed.

One thing that became apparent as we were writing these lessons is that in no way are we able to include all that we would like in each one. Had we done that, the book would have become an encyclopedia and then we still may have omitted important information.

Please use this as a guide, interject your thoughts and work diligently at improving your company. If you do that, we will have succeeded in our goal of providing a handbook for effective supervision. Read, enjoy and LEARN.

LESSON 1

DEFINING SUPERVISION

In writing a book about supervision it is probably prudent to begin with a definition so let's begin by offering TWO definitions. First let's use the dictionary definition:

THE ACTION OR PROCESS OF WATCHING AND DIRECTING WHAT SOMEONE DOES OR HOW SOMETHING IS DONE. (The action or process of supervising someone or something).

The key word as I see it in this definition is directing. In our industry we generally employ supervisors to direct staff members to do the work assigned in the manner in which the organization has established it to be done.

Now let me provide a simpler and more direct definition for a Building Service Contractor supervisor and other service companies.

GETTING A QUALITY JOB DONE WITH EFFECTIVE AND EFFICIENT SYSTEMATIC PROCESSES AND PROCEDURES THAT PRODUCE HIGH SATISFACTION FOR THE CUSTOMER AND THE BUDGETED PROFIT FOR THE COMPANY.

The second definition can be rather imposing but isn't that what we ask our supervisors to do every day or night out on the job? It isn't good enough just to do the specifications we are handed because a lot more goes into the job than that.

Richard D. Ollek, CBSE, RGC

In addition, we ask our supervisors to bring every job in on budget—even if the sales department priced it wrong. Most of the time, the sales department says they have allowed more than enough time to do the job and operations says they need a lot more additional time. Ever happened in your company? Sure did in mine.

You will notice I used the words systematic processes and procedures in my definition and much of this book will be devoted to providing guidance on those systematic processes and procedures. That is why we titled the book The Handbook for Effective Supervision.

One more thing before we move on to the next lesson that I think is a critical dynamic that each company must subscribe to in order to be successful and that is the difference between providing customer service according to the specifications and providing customer satisfaction. Let me define the differences,

CUSTOMER SERVICE is a concept. Everyone says they provide or want to provide customer service and that is an admirable quality to have. But have you ever lost a customer where you felt you were doing everything in the specifications? The customer must just be unreasonable because I bet no one else can keep that building as clean as we have. Sound familiar? Many companies, in fact, employ customer service representatives that visit the buildings and attempt to make sure the customer is "happy". That brings me to that statement that Tom Peters, one of the best known management gurus said many years ago, "If you have to have a customer service representative in your company, what are the rest of the people doing"? I subscribe wholeheartedly to that theory. We should all be in the customer service business. Shouldn't all of the people working in our company be able to encounter a customer and have the training in how to communicate properly with that customer?

Now let me define customer satisfaction,

CUSTOMER SATISFACTION is a demonstration of customer service. You see, there is much more that goes into keeping a customer than cleaning according to the specifications every day or night. Everything we do or don't do that affects that customers opinion of our company is what demonstrates customer satisfaction or lack of it.

As we continue on with these lessons, we will endeavor to make clear what some of those "things" we do or don't do are and how they affect our customer retention.

There is no question that the supervisors in the organization have a highly important, responsible position and it is incumbent on every company to make the right hiring decision and then make sure those people hired have the training and support to satisfy the customer and bring every job in on budget.

That brings me to an error that many companies commit when placing a person in this important position of supervising and that is promoting a great cleaning technician to the position of supervisor. Being a great cleaning technician does not necessarily translate into being a great supervisor. The fact that they know how to clean does not translate in to knowing how to supervise. As we work our way through the lessons in this book, it will become very apparent. Don't make the mistake of promoting someone just because they know how to clean or because they have been with you for a long time. Many great cleaning technicians have been promoted to the position of supervisor only to be promoted to their level of incompetence. They many times can't do the job and then either quit or are terminated and we lose on both fronts—we lose a great cleaning tech and we still don't have a qualified supervisor. Just a word to the wise.

Now before I get all the great cleaning technicians angry at me, let me say that many cleaning technicians have become effective supervisors but their success rate is not high.

Please answer and discuss the following questions before going to lesson 2.

1. What other definitions of supervision do you have?

2. Describe a time when you lost a customer and you felt you were doing everything in the specifications.

3. What has been your best and worst experience as a supervisor?

4. Have you ever had a building that you thought was dirty but the customer told you everything looked great? Why do you think they said that?

LESSON 2

IT'S THE SAME, ONLY DIFFERENT

While the dictionary definition of supervision hasn't changed, nor has mine, the way of effectively supervising has changed. As you weave your way through these lessons you will become very aware of some of those changes and hopefully will recognize additional changes not mentioned in these lessons.

Let's look at how business has changed over the past several years that has necessitated how a supervisor must change if they are to be effective.

In the "olden" days, sales were made with a handshake and "we'll take care of your facility" attitude. The supervisor could just keep everything in their head because, after all, they were to keep the facility clean.

From a sales standpoint, prospects were interested in "do you know how to clean, can you strip and recoat a tile floor, can you shampoo carpets, wash windows etc.? Do you have the expertise to perform all of these tasks"?

You see, back then, and I'll let you define back then, the main focus was always on do you know how to clean?

I can remember some of the "old timers" telling me how they would price a proposal. You find out how much the customer will pay and then you spend half of that on labor to do the job. Then you spend 25% on supplies and the 25% left over was for overhead and profit. Times have changed, haven't they?

Now let's fast forward to today. If you have been invited to present a proposal for cleaning (not a bid), the prospect assumes you already know how to clean or you probably wouldn't be there in the first place.

So, what do most astute buyers of service today want to know from a prospective vendor? Let's list a few and see if you can think of any additional ones.

- What kind of training program do you have?

- We want to visit one of your training sessions.

- We require background checks.

- We require drug screening of all vendor employees.

- What is your safety record? We need to know your "mod" factor.

- What sort of quality control program do you have?

- What is the pay scale of your employees?

- What sort of benefit package do you offer your employees?

- What kind of quality review meetings do you conduct with your clients? How often?

- What technology do you provide that enables us to track your quality and work progress?

- Do all of your employees speak English? If not, how do you handle our communication with them and their communication with us?

- We want a full disclosure proposal so we know how much time you plan to spend in our facility and how much overhead and profit you plan on having.

If you are a business owner or sales representative reading this you can probably add significantly to this list.

Looking at these points and thinking back, it is obvious that an effective supervisor can no longer just commit everything to memory and hope to pass it on to the next person when they quit or retire. It's not only about cleaning anymore.

So, how does a supervisor today truly become an effective supervisor? There are many great tools available that can really enhance your ability and your favorability with the customer.

With companies like Team, Cleantelligent, Chronotek, Express Time, Janitorial Manager, Paperless Proposal etc. taking the lead in technology, the task becomes much simpler. But we have to start with the basic information so these great vendors can really help us.

On the pages that follow is a sample client information form that I consider to be essential for every effective supervisor to have in their possession at all times. With the modern technology available today, it can be put on a tablet and referred to when needed. It also can then be updated as changes occur with a client. Take the time now to review this information.

Client Information

District Name:
Job Name:

Today's Date

Job #: **Customer #:**
Date to Start

Action Form Completed by
Sales Representative
Operations Approved by
Corporate Approved by

Billing Information

Customer Contact
Contact Title
Contact Phone
Contact Fax
Contact E-mail
Bill to:
Name
Street
Street
City
State   Zip

Purchase Order Number:
Purchase Order Start Date:
Purchase Order End Date:

Special Billing Instructions:

Service Location Information

Job Location
Street
Street
City
State   Zip

Contact Person #1 Name
Contact Person #1 Title
Contact Person #1 Phone
Contact Person #1 Fax
Contact Person #1 E-Mail
Contact Person #2 Name
Contact Person #2 Title
Contact Person #2 Phone
Contact Person #2 Fax
Contact Person #2 E-Mail

Alarm Company
Alarm Company Phone
Security Code Number

Alarm System: Yes
                       No

Alarm Location:

Original Keys Issued - Total
Original Keys Given to

Location of Trash Dumpster:

Entry & Key to Use:

Location of Log Book:

Location of Water Supply:

Location of Supply Room:

Location of Water Disposal:

Location of Breakers:

Earliest Start Time: Latest Completion Time:

Number of Customer
Employees at Facility

Notes:

Description of Job Site

Client Information

District Name:

Job Name: Today's Date

Special Cleaning Areas of Interest	
Item 1	
Item 2	
Item 3	
Item 4	
Item 5	

Specifications
TEAM Cleaning Plan

Plus Tasks in Addition to Our TEAM Cleaning Plan	
Item 1	
Item 2	
Item 3	
Item 4	
Item 5	
Item 6	
Item 7	

Minus Tasks Included to Our TEAM Cleaning Plan	
Item 1	
Item 2	
Item 3	
Item 4	
Item 5	
Item 6	
Item 7	

Project Work (Include information such as Strip & Wax - number of coats of seal, number of coats of finish. Scrub and wax - number of coats of finish. Carpet Cleaning - Rotary & extract, Extract only, or Bonnet clean. PLEASE LIST MONTHS THAT WORK SHOULD BE DONE FOR WORK TICKET PURPOSES.

Item 1	
Item 2	
Item 3	
Item 4	
Item 5	
Item 6	
Item 7	
Item 8	

Quads	
Quad 1	
Quad 2	
Quad 3	
Quad 4	

Notes

Client Information

District Name: [   ]

Job Name: [   ]   **Today's Date** [   ]

TEAM Cleaning Frequency (check days of service)								Notes
Sun	Mon	Tues	Wed	Thur	Fri	Sat	Holiday	

Will this be a Route Job? (check block)   No [   ]   or   Yes [   ]   If Yes complete route travel section

Description	Route Travel Section (For TEAM Cleaning)	Travel For Project Work Item 1	Travel For Project Work Item 2	Travel For Project Work Item 3
Number of Staff required to perform work:	Each	Each	Each	Each
Travel time to job	Minutes	Minutes	Minutes	Minutes
Unload equipment and set up time for job	Minutes	Minutes	Minutes	Minutes
Loading equipment after job complete	Minutes	Minutes	Minutes	Minutes
Travel time to next job or office	Minutes	Minutes	Minutes	Minutes

Resale Items (List and place a check mark in proper block)							
Product	Product Code	Type Size	Customer Furnish	Janitorial Furnish	Janitorial Resale	Stock Level	Notes
Toilet Tissue							
Paper Towels							
Hand Soap							
Sanitary Napkins							
Tampons							
Seat Covers							
Light Bulbs							
Small Liners							
Medium Liners							
Large Liners							
Other Instructions							

Authorized Supply Items						
Janitorial Item Code #	Item Description	Unit or Size (ea.,gal., etc.)	Quantity to be kept on hand	Reorder Level:	Resale Yes/No	Notes
Products approved by:					Date:	

Client Information

District Name: _____

Job Name: _____   **Today's Date** _____

Equipment to be left at job site

Quantity	Item Description	Notes
	Backpack	
	Trash Barrel	
	Mop Bucket w/Wringer	
	Maid Cart	
	Quikfill Station	
	Buffer	
	Burnisher	
	Auto Scrubber	
	Carpet Extractor	
	Wet Vacuum	
	14E Scrubber	

Window Cleaning Schedule

Will this contract include window cleaning: Check   Yes _____   Or   No _____

Inside	Outside	Frequency	Months	Notes
		WEEKLY		
		EVERY OTHER WEEK		
		MONTHLY		
		QUARTERLY		

Comments:

Windows Count (North side of facility)

	4X8	4X4	2X8			ENTRY DOOR	Notes
Ground Level							
Second Story							
Partition Glass							
High Glass							

Windows Count (South side of facility)

	4X8	4X4	2X8		OTHER	ENTRY DOOR	Notes
Ground Level							
Second Story							
Partition Glass							
High Glass							

Windows count (East side of facility)

	4X8	4X4	2X8			ENTRY DOOR	Notes
Ground Level							
Second Story							
Partition Glass							
High Glass							

Client Information

District Name:

Job Name: **Today's Date**

Windows Count (West side of facility)

	4X8	4X4	2X8		ENTRY DOOR	Notes
Ground Level						
Second Story						
Partition Glass						
High Glass						

Comments:

Window Pricing

Frequency	Janitorial Price/Trip	Sub-Contractor's Price/Trip	Notes
WEEKLY			
EVERY OTHER WEEK			
2 TIMES MONTHLY			
MONTHLY			
QUARTERLY			

Mat Schedule

Will this contract include Mat Rental: Check   Yes   Or   No

Mat Sizes: 3X4, 3X5, 4X6, 3X10   Other   **Colors:** Midnight Grey, Casino Red, Taupe and Walnut

Standard Mats

Size	Qty	Color	Price	Frequency	Location	Notes

Comments:

Special Order Mats

Size	Qty	Color	Price	Frequency	Location	Notes

Comments:

Client Information

District Name:

Job Name: **Today's Date**

Teleteam

Location of Telephones for Clock-In / Out

Telephone Number	Telephone Number	Telephone Number	Telephone Number

Instructions for setting up TeleTeam in blocks below

1. **Times:** Enter the start and end time that you will allow our staff to clock in. Multiple periods or shifts are allowed
2. **Number of staff:** Enter the number of staff required in the blocks below the days of the week

1. Times		2. Number of staff on this shift								
Start time	End time	Sun	Mon	Tues	Wed	Thur	Fri	Sat	Holiday	Notes

Do you want the system to page a Janitorial Representative for absences:
    Check   Yes [ ]   or   No [ ]

If yes, List Janitorial Representative to be paged:

What is Pager number:

If this is a set schedule shift i.e. 8 am to 5 pm and you do not want any one to clock in or out
before or after this scheduled time check   Yes [ ]   Or   No [ ]

What is the lunch time you want automatically deducted? [ ] Minutes

Key Controls					
Keys	Original	Made	Total	Code #	Location & Notes
Alarm			0		
Sanitary			0		
Tissue			0		
Towels			0		
Entry			0		
			0		
			0		

Client Information

District Name:

Job Name:

Today's Date

As you reviewed the information you no doubt found information that doesn't apply to your organization, like mat service, which our company provided. You also probably have information not included that needs to be added. That's great. The form is only a template and our hope here is that you will adapt it to your company and make it an integral part of effective supervision.

In fact, it is my guess that many companies already have a template they have designed for their own organization and that's wonderful. This form is shown only as an example. Do you have one? Are you using it? If you don't have one, why not?

A couple of items that, that appear minor and can become major we found particularly helpful to record on the form were,

1. Location of dumpsters--We learned this the hard way. Dumping trash seems simple enough but that first night when you get ready to take out the trash and find the dumpster 50 yards from the back door you just added several minutes to the time for servicing that facility. Fifteen minutes here and fifteen minutes there and pretty soon you are talking big bucks. (More on this in a later lesson).

2. Location of the breakers--Many times service providers want to make a first time great impression on the new client and will decide to burnish the lobby floors to return them to a shining "wow" when the new client arrives the next day. It can be embarrassing when that breaker is blown and we have to call the new client at home asking where the breaker is located.

Both of these examples seem minor in themselves until they happen to you. Do the Boy Scout thing, be prepared and save yourself a lot of grief and embarrassment, not to mention creating doubt in the mind of your new client as to the correctness of their decision to hire your company.

As you review this lesson, ask yourself the following questions,

1. Have I ever had a new customer call the day after we began the first day of service with a complaint about how we performed the first day?

2. Have I ever not had information about a customer when I needed it on the job?

3. What tools do I need to become a more effective supervisor, especially in starting a new customer?

4. Do we have all the information we need on all of our customers in one place where we can access it immediately if need be?

5. If the answer to number 4 is no, what are we going to do about it?

LESSON 3

THE MANY HATS OF A SUPERVISOR

An effective, efficient, well trained supervisor has numerous duties that have to be performed on a daily basis. They have several "hats" they have to wear to do their job of satisfying the customer and bringing the accounts in on budget.

In this lesson we want to review these various hats and discuss the difficult tasks associated with them. The first hat is,

"FIREMAN"

This is one of the most important and yet dreaded hats that a good supervisor has to wear. It seems every day brings a new adventure with an emergency that needs immediate attention. Examples can be that someone didn't do the job they were supposed to do the previous night and now we have an unhappy customer and much of the next service is taken correcting the issue and hoping we can get the customer back in our good graces. Ever had that happen? It is critical that a good supervisor can address these issues in a calm and professional manner.

What about a situation where an emergency develops in a facility and we have to take quick, prompt action? An example might be a water leak that disrupts the entire planned evening of work. It has to be taken care of and all the other work scheduled for the shift still has to be done.

How important is this? My company obtained a very sizable contract when a prospect we had been working on called me on Christmas Eve to request help on a major water leak in their facility.

We sprung into action and were able to assist this prospect who then awarded us the contract effective January 1—a week later.

Why did they call us? In the janitor's closet were three telephone numbers of our competitor to be called in the event of an emergency. My new customer told me that when they called, one number had been disconnected, the other one was of an individual no longer with that company and the third number had no answer and no answering machine to leave a message.

We'll discuss more on this in a later lesson.

As we discuss the fireman hat of a supervisor, we must have a person who can create quick and innovative solutions to issues and emergencies and put out fires that present themselves. It's one thing to be available on a moments notice, it's another thing to know what to do when that issue or emergency arises. If you are a supervisor reading this, do you know what to do in the event of a major accident like a water leak that may occur in one of your facilities? If not, maybe more training may be in order. If you are an owner or other top manager, it may be wise to make sure what your company procedure is for such an incident. Who gets called, who are the backup staff members, is someone always available to assist a customer in an emergency?

I always found it interesting that major emergencies always seem to occur on a holiday like Thanksgiving, Christmas or New Year. Probably isn't really the case but always seemed that way.

The second hat is,

"POLICE OFFICER"

This hat is one that many supervisors also dread wearing. It entails some of those tasks that many of us hate to face such as,

- Making sure all the work gets done

- Making sure all procedures are followed

- Conducting discipline promptly and properly

The Guide to Effective Supervision

None of these are very exciting are they? Let's look at each one of them.

Making sure all the work gets done is a massive responsibility. One of the issues that makes it so daunting is the fact that every day/night can present a new set of problems/opportunities. You see, as a supervisor you don't just tell someone to get the job done, you have to MAKE SURE it gets done which can mean following up late and maybe not getting off exactly when you thought you would.

I once had an Operations Manager that felt if he told someone to do the job, his responsibility ended. After hearing him tell me that several times when work had not been done properly and the customers were calling the second and third time on the same issues, I reminded him that if all he was going to do was tell someone else to get the job done, I didn't need him. I could do that without a messenger. Well, the situation continued and I ended up taking him to lunch and buying his to go. He just didn't get it.

I found this area of responsibility to be one of the most difficult for supervisors to conquer. We usually hire them for a general shift of say, 3 PM to 11 PM and many have trouble adapting to the fact that you get to go home when the work in your area is satisfactorily completed and NOT BEFORE. That may be 2 in the morning or it may be when the sun comes up. If you are a supervisor reading this, take heed. Remember our definition of supervision discussed in lesson 1? We talked about customer satisfaction with no mention of hours needed to provide that satisfaction.

The second bullet point of making sure all procedures are followed can also be somewhat disconcerting. Many times if a building is short of staff or training of new people is taking more time than you feel you have, the tendency can be to try some shortcuts to get the work done. A reminder here might be in order that the customer is paying for a complete job as was promised in the sales presentation, not shortcuts. Don't forget if you are developing shortcuts and not following the procedures as outlined by your organization, what you have effectively done is created new "shortcut" procedures that all of a sudden become the company's standard procedure and soon we are wondering why so many complaints are being called or emailed into the office. So, as a

19

police officer supervisor you have the responsibility to MAKE SURE ALL PROPER PROCDEDURES ARE FOLLOWED ALL OF THE TIME.

Conducting discipline properly and promptly when necessary is another of the police office hat duties that a supervisor has to perform. We are not going to spend time here talking about this important hat as we are devoting an entire lesson to this important and many times unpleasant task.

The third hat a supervisor must wear is that of,

"COACH"

Here are some of the duties that a coach/supervisor must perform,

- Be able to train/retrain the staff members as required to assure customer satisfaction. I am hopeful that your company has a thorough, detailed new employee orientation AND initial training program so new people go out to the field with at least a basic understanding of who your company is and how to do the basics of their responsibility. If your company doesn't have this important piece then let me suggest you develop it NOW—not soon—NOW.

- Sending new employees out to work with an "experienced" team member to "learn" the ropes" is not a good orientation and training program. That new employee may just learn the duties wrong from that experienced member of the team and the ropes they learn may just be the ropes that hang them. More on the training issue in a later lesson. (Not going to tell you which lesson because I want you to read the whole book).

As a coach it is the supervisor's responsibility to always be retraining staff members on how to perform the tasks assigned. We all are human and we get into bad habits of doing things and have to be continually reminded of the established procedure. Most people want to do the job correctly and many times it's just a matter of reminding them what your company procedures are.

A supervisor/coach also has the responsibility of training all members in their area on how to use new products and equipment that the company may want to incorporate into the cleaning procedures.

- Always being able to encourage the staff is a very important part of the supervisor/coach responsibility. Many times the only encouragement or positive words a person may hear will come from their supervisor. They may have been fighting bill collectors or their spouse or have a child discipline issue and it can be the highlight of their day to hear their supervisor say "great job" or "keep up the good work" etc.

Keep one thing in mind though on this issue. Most of us can recognize false or fake statements. Employees know when what you are telling them is from the heart or just some fancy learned phrase of praise. Say it when you mean it and mean it when you say it.

Scheduling or rescheduling work is another important assignment that a great supervisor/coach has to have. Almost every day a supervisor will encounter a building that has a staff shortage or staff change that requires thinking fast on their feet and being able to assign the needed duties and train where necessary to get the job done on budget and to the customers satisfaction. We will address more on this issue in a later lesson as well.

- Being able to effectively communicate with different cultures and different generations in today's business world is, without a doubt, one of the most important characteristics needed. Different generations grew up with different ideas and sometimes different morals and as the internet expands and shrinks our world, more and more different cultures are entering the workforce and I believe this is a good thing. It is a good thing for your company only if you will take the time to understand what all of these differences are and are able to mold and manage them into an effective team and efficient company.

I have long been a believer that we need all types of different people to create a successful organization. For years I had the good fortune of working with a work force in the Southwest USA that spoke only

Spanish and the quality of their work was outstanding. Even though I did not speak Spanish we were able to communicate in a way that satisfied our customers. Our annual summer company family picnics were one of the highlights of the year along with our Christmas visit from a Spanish speaking Santa Claus.

Here again, because of the importance of this issue, we are devoting an entire lesson in this book to working with generational and cultural differences in the workplace. If you haven't already done so, I suggest you embrace this opportunity to move your company forward in a positive manner.

There is no question that today's younger generation is thinking differently than those of us born prior to 1946. Being one of those old traditionalists, I have had to adjust to the different generations in a lot of ways. This is by no means a complaint as I have learned so much by trying to understand where each of the generations is coming from. It doesn't mean I necessarily agree with all their ideas and viewpoints but it does give me a better understanding where they are coming from. I just learned that LOL does not stand for lots of licorice. As stated earlier, an entire lesson in this book is dedicated to the generational and cultural differences in the workplace.

The fourth hat that an effective supervisor must wear is,

"AMBASSADOR"

This is one that many times is difficult for a supervisor to master. (Not that any of us ever really MASTER it). Why? Let's look at some of the duties of the Ambassador hat.

- Being a peacekeeper in the organization or at least in the area the supervisor is responsible for is not an easy task. This hat requires you to fully understand all company policies and be able to communicate them to your staff in a way that reinforces what the organization is attempting to accomplish.

If you don't agree with a policy, you don't make a statement like "I don't agree with top management but that's the way it is". Learn why the policy is what it is and conduct your business in a supportive manner.

- As an ambassador you will be called on to settle disputes among your workforce. Some of these are simple and require only an explanation and sometimes you will have to take some unpleasant action with certain staff members. This can border sometimes on the Police Officer hat but if you are an effective supervisor you should be able to switch hats without much difficulty.

- As a supervisor wearing the Ambassador hat you have a major responsibility to always represent your company in a professional manner when dealing with a customer.

Remember that the customer is the reason we are in business and their satisfaction has to be the top priority of the organization. More customers are lost through poor customer relationship skills than through poor service or price considerations.

With that in mind it is incumbent that every organization has a planned continuing education program for supervisors and that they make a commitment to spend time improving their relationship skills. It is a proven fact, if you will spend 20 minutes per day learning something additional about your position, that in 5 years you will be considered one of the experts in your field. Think about it, only 20 minutes a day. Check out what you have done for the last week and I will bet you that you could find 20 minutes in each of those days to learn more about the great industry you are in and how you can become better at what you do.

- Here is an important part of the Ambassador hat. NEVER MAKE EXCUSES TO THE CUSTOMER. If you are visiting with a customer about a cleaning or employee issue, never say things like,

  o I told the people to do it.
  o I just don't have enough time to do it.

- o   Our equipment was broke.
- o   I just can't find good help.
- o   The company, they.
- o   I have been so busy.

And the list goes on. Can you add some to this list? When you make statements like these you are telling the customer it isn't your fault and you are trying to blame someone or something for not satisfying them. You are the supervisor of the account and if it isn't your fault, whose fault is it?

Look at the list again. Did you tell the people and then didn't follow up? As to time allotments and equipment issues, that is a discussion for supervision and company management, not supervision and customer management.

The same goes for the bad help excuse. That is an internal issue that should NEVER be discussed with a customer.

Let's talk a bit about "the company, they". Who is the company? It is YOU and all of the other employees in the organization. When you say something like "the company they" you are implying that you are not part of the company. If you are being paid every payday, you are part of the company and should be leaving the "they" out of the conversation.

Also, when you tell a customer that you have been busy, you are leaving the impression with that customer that they are not as important to you as other customers. EVERY customer should be treated as if they are the only customer you have.

The fifth hat is,

"ACCOUNTANT"

- • An effective supervisor must make sure that all paperwork/ computer reports are accurate and turned in ON TIME. Today's supervisor has to have the knowledge and understanding of computers and all the other electronic gadgetry that comes with satisfying the customer and bringing the accounts in on budget. This is where some of the generational differences can arise. The older generation just wants to get the job done and explain it while the younger generations want to look at it on the screen. A word to all you traditionalists and baby boomers if you haven't already figured it out, we live in a computer age. Boy, was that an obvious statement.

We'll talk more technology when we get into training but I have seen more than I can count, supervisors leave or being asked to leave their job because they will not adapt to modern technology. Such a waste of talent. Many of them knew everything about cleaning but would not embrace this aspect of their position.

We now are delivering sales proposals on line, and companies like Team Software, CleanTelligent, and Janitorial Manager have simplified the reporting processes of different departments within the company and it is critically important that supervisors learn to use all of the tools that can make their job so much easier and efficient.

I can remember our supervisors laboring over paper timesheets and how they had difficulty getting all the paperwork in on time. With today's telephone timekeeping systems, it can free the supervisor up to do more training of the staff or remember the 20 minute suggestion?

- The accountant hat entails numerous other obvious items such as making sure labor, equipment, and supply budgets are on track, quality is maintained, inspections with or without the customer are done, and then taking action on any issues that need to be addressed.

So there you have what I consider the 5 major hats an effective and successful supervisor must wear every day on the job. In other words, the supervisor has the responsibility to create an environment of success in their assigned area. That means,

- NEVER QUIT LEARNING.

- ASK FOR HELP IN AREAS YOU ARE NOT AS STRONG AS YOU NEED TO BE.

- TAKE RESPONSIBILITY FOR YOUR LEARNING, DON'T WAIT ON OTHERS BUT ALWAYS ATTEND ANY LEARNING OPPORTUNITY YOUR COMPANY PRESENTS.

- TAKE RESPONSIBILITY FOR YOUR OWN ACTIONS.

So let me suggest you take a few minutes to review this lesson and see where improvement needs to be made and then answer the following questions,

1. Where do I need to improve?

2. Where do I plan to get that help?

3. Which hat is the most difficult for me?

4. Who can help me become better at wearing that hat?

In the next lesson we are going to address the traits needed to become a successful supervisor.

LESSON 4

BUILDING THE PERFECT SUPERVISOR

Hopefully by now you have learned how important and valuable good supervisors are to an organization. They are the daily contact with all the line people and many times, actually most of the time, they are the front line of communication with the customers.

So far we have defined what a supervisor is using the dictionary definition and then using my own definition.

We have discussed the various "hats" a supervisor must wear on a daily basis if they are to perform their job satisfactorily. Based on those hats and our definition, the next step is to determine what characteristics to look for in a good supervisor.

Whenever I do a supervisor's workshop or seminar, one of the first exercises we have all participants do is define what they consider to be the traits of a perfect supervisor. We ask them to build a perfect supervisor, if you will. This really is a great exercise for getting everyone thinking and involved. Try it in your company to see what your group is thinking.

At this point I want to list what I consider to be the critical ones every good supervisor must have, so here we go,

- HONESTY---It is my belief if the supervisor isn't honest, all of the rest of the traits really don't matter. Agree?

A few years I ago I was doing this exercise with a group at a conference and we were filling up several pages and hanging them on the wall when an elderly gentlemen stood up in the back of the room and said that we had missed the most important trait, that being honesty. He said that if he couldn't trust someone to be honest in all their dealings representing his company the rest of the traits didn't matter. Pretty profound isn't it? He was absolutely correct and honesty heads my list above all other traits. The rest of the traits we list here all tie for second place. Read all of them and see in what order you would put them.

- SELF STARTER---The supervisor is managing an area of the company and if he or she has to be told to get moving or what their entire schedule for the day has to be, we probably have the wrong person in the position.

- TAKES RESPONSIBILITY FOR THEIR OWN ACTIONS---We seem to live in a society where every one blames someone else when something goes wrong. A good supervisor will admit when they make a mistake and take corrective action to learn how not to make that mistake again.

- GOOD COMMUNICATOR---This is an extremely important trait because of the diversity of the work force today. We talked a bit about that in the previous lesson and will address it again later, but being able to communicate in a positive, understandable, level headed way is extremely important.

- SAFETY CONSCIOUS---Many supervisors are unaware of the importance of safety in the workplace. A company's workers compensation insurance rate is dependent on the safety of its workforce. With a good safety record a company can many times cut its workers compensation premium in half while a disregard for safety can double a company's rate. Since workers compensation premiums are based on total payroll dollars this can amount to a substantial amount of premium dollars each year.

I have talked about the financial hit a company can take in insurance premiums if they don't pay attention to safety, but let's look at the price we pay by having employees off of work with an injury.

If someone is injured on the job, we are now faced with finding someone to train in that position and the supervisor has to spend hours making sure that new employee not only knows how to do the work properly but what the specifics are of the facility they are working in. It just adds more hours to an already full workload that the supervisor has. So we have a double negative if we don't pay close attention to safety. Oh, and I forgot, there are mounds of paperwork and reports to complete if an employee is injured on the job. More hours spent.

Let's not forget the impact an injury has on the employee. It affects their family if job time is lost not to mention if it forces them to also be absent from their full time job if this is a supplemental job for them.

- ABLE TO MAKE QUICK DECISIONS---One thing I learned early on in business as a supervisor was that I can have the best planned out day and when I get to work something has come up that changes the schedule. A good supervisor has to address those issues and still be able to accomplish the planned schedule they had for that day and---do it effectively and efficiently.

- ABLE TO MEET DEADLINES---There are all kinds of deadlines that need to be met every day. We have customers that need special attention for an event they have coming up while payroll for our company has to be approved at the same time. Then we learn that some of our employees will not be at work today and we have to have that special project done by a certain time. This trait goes hand in hand with the ability to make quick decisions discussed in the previous paragraphs.

- EXCELLENT TRAINER---One of the most important and maybe the most frequent duties of a good supervisor is the ability to train new employees and retrain existing ones. Not having this characteristic can really damage your company's image and lose customers. A critical trait to have and if you are a supervisor and don't have that trait work hard to develop it

NOW. We will be devoting a lesson later in this book on how people learn and how you can do effective training.

- AGREE WITH AND SUPPORT COMPANY CULTURE---It is important that the whole team is on board with the culture of the company and presents a united front to employees and customers at all times. You know your company culture, understand what is expected to support that culture and if a supervisor cannot endorse that culture, whatever it may be, that supervisor should leave the organization. We are assuming here that every company reading this is an honest, upstanding, corporate citizen that believes in doing the right thing in all business dealings with customers and employees.

- KNOWS ALL THE TECHNICAL ASPECTS OF THE JOB---I can remember interviewing prospective managers who told me they didn't need to know how to do the work but they knew how to manage and, after all, wasn't that what I was interviewing for? I was interviewing for a manager but I strongly believe if a person is going to be in the field managing people, they need to understand what the job entails of the people they are supervising. They don't necessarily need to be an expert at it but the do need to know the basics. If you don't know the system of Team Cleaning for example, how will you be able to train and retrain the troops in your area? You have to believe whatever they tell you on procedure and time because YOU DON'T KNOW. Learn all the technical aspects and remember to spend that 20 minutes a day and you will become the expert in your field.

- BASIC UNDERSTANDING OF MATH---Today, more than ever, supervisors are being asked to understand the budgets that they are being tasked with. Know what the budget numbers mean and if you don't know, ask! I held weekly budget meeting with the area supervisors to review their numbers and to make sure they understood them and how they could impact them. (Had fun doing this because I couldn't always speak the language but we also used the time to each learn a new word of the other person's language).

- HAVE BASIC COMPUTER SKILLS---This trait is really important today as most quality inspection programs are internet based as are many training programs. In addition, a large number of applications are now submitted on line. Recently, I had a client that had to terminate a supervisor because she refused to become at least somewhat proficient on a computer and she did not want to become a line worker in the company. My client offered to pay the tuition for her to go to school and pay her for her time in class but she would not do it. Get the skills necessary because it becomes more important as time goes by.

Well, there you have some of the basic traits required to build a perfect supervisor. When we do this exercise in my workshops we generally can list 25 to 30 without to much difficulty. How many more can you list? How about taking out a piece of paper and pencil and write down the ones you can think of that are not listed here. It's a great thinking exercise.

As we close out this chapter, let me suggest you do the following exercises to help you become a better supervisor.

1. As a follow up to the suggestion above, list all the additional traits of an effective supervisor that we did not mention in this lesson.

2. List those traits from our list and the ones you made that you need to learn more about to become a better supervisor.

3. Write down where, when, and how you plan to get the knowledge needed to keep improving.

LESSON 5

CUSTOMER RELATIONS TRAINING

The area of customer relations is an extremely important one for supervisors because as I mentioned in an earlier lesson, once sales has left the scene, the supervisor and the line workers/cleaning techs will many times have more interaction/communication with the customer than anyone else in the organization.

How the supervisor handles the situation can be the difference of retaining or losing a customer. It's vital the supervisors know how they are to respond or react in each situation.

Let me begin with my definition of customer relations,

EVERYTHING WE DO, OR DON'T DO, THAT AFFECTS THE CUSTOMERS IMPRESSION OF OUR COMPANY

That's a pretty wide and all encompassing definition but it has to be. Our company is on display and being judged in everything we do. To demonstrate what I mean I want you to do the exercise below that should help to clarify the definition of customer relations.

EXERCISE

Think of a situation where you have had bad service, maybe in a restaurant, a dry cleaners, car repair shop, grocery store etc. Then answer these questions,

1. How did you feel?

2. Was your problem resolved?

3. Did you go back to the place?

4. Did you tell others?

5. If you told others, how many did you tell?

Do you now feel good about that experience or do you still harbor bad thoughts about them? See how it could relate to your organization?

Statistics have shown that 93% of unhappy customers never complain. My best example of this is my wife who when she gets a bad meal in a restaurant will tell me how terrible it is but when the waiter or manager asks "how's your meal?" she will, without exception, tell them it is good. I, on the other hand, will tell them if I am not happy and have been known to embarrass my dear wife and that may be part of the reason she hesitates to complain.

To take it to the next step of statistics, 90% of unhappy customers never come back. Ever wonder why there is such a high casualty rate among restaurants? They have to get the food AND service right or they are gone.

Going another step further, each unhappy customer tells 9 others and 13% of unhappy customers tell 20 others.

Keeping these daunting statistics in mind, let's develop a list of those things that we do or don't do that affects a customers impression of our company. I am not going to list them in any particular order but after you read my list and add to it, see if you can place them in the order you would want them for your company.

1. Our own personal appearance—How you dress has a tremendous impact on our customers. I mean from making sure you take a bath every day to making sure you have on a clean set of clothes/uniform every day. How's your grooming? I know that we all have our individuality but it is important to understand

the feelings of your customers and see if your individuality would in any way offend them, If so, think you ought to make adjustments? During the 70's I had a supervisor who refused to cut his hair even though the customer he serviced was an older gentlemen (and our largest account) who was dead set against them "hippie" types. I bought my supervisor a hair net and a cap to wear during business hours and everybody peacefully co-existed.

2. The appearance of our equipment. Can you even read the name of the brand or is it covered with stripper water and floor finish? In a restaurant, if the customers can see the cooking area, what impression does that leave?

3. The company vehicles. I always find it somewhat disconcerting that some of the dirtiest vehicles I see on the streets are those of the people whose job it is to keep things clean---the janitorial service company's. What kind of impression does that leave, not only to the customer that may see the vehicle, but also to the prospect that may be searching for a new company? Would they call your company? I am always amazed at how many phone numbers on the side or back of a van have one or more numbers missing. Now there's a great advertising opportunity---not! It was our company policy that every vehicle was washed every Friday, period. Oh, and how does the inside of the vehicle look? McDonald or Wendy's wrappers come flying out when you open the door?

4. How about when a supervisor or other employee complains about the company to or in front of a customer? Statements like "they don't give me enough time" or "my equipment is always broken down" or "I can't seem to get them to give me a raise" or "that's not in the specs" if asked to do a small favor for the customer, are all statements that leave an unfavorable impression of our company.

5. Sitting down on the job is one that usually will generate comments from the customer when we are asking for an increase in the monthly investment from the customer. My suggestion

is that whatever your break or lunch schedule is, you should always have the group take it together. When a customer walks through the facility at different times of the day or night and sees one of our employees here and another there sitting down at different times they can get the impression that we are just sitting down on the job when, in fact, the employee may really be entitled to the break. Save having to defend it, just have everyone take the break at the same time in the same place.

6. Knowing what to do in unusual situations such as security, plumbing, and electrical issues. This doesn't mean you have to be a security guard, plumber or electrician but it does mean a good supervisor should know the procedure to follow in the event any of these should occur.

7. Being honest in all of our dealing is a very important thing to do all of the time. Admitting to our mistakes and assuring the customer any issue that may arise will be promptly taken care of is one of those things that we do that leaves a favorable impression with the customer. One important thing to remember is that the customer is always the customer and is to be satisfied. Someone once told me that even if the customer is wrong they are always the customer and are to be treated with utmost respect. The ownership will determine if the customer is too unreasonable to work with, but until that decision is made the supervisor must always treat the customer in a positive polite manner.

8. Knowing how to clean to the specifications designed for that particular customer is also something that we do that affects the customer's impression of our company. Doing EVERYTHING that has been promised is the right thing to do—No short cuts.

9. Having a positive attitude toward our employees is critical. We send a positive message to our customer when we support our employees and if they are not doing the job correctly a good supervisor should conduct training to help them do the job correctly. Our internal difficulties should always remain internal and we should always have a positive attitude when addressing a customer. They want to have the assurance that the

company they hired to provide their service was a wise decision. Complaining about the work or employees or customers only sends a negative message to the customer and encourages them to seek another vendor to perform the work.

10. Always have a neat and clean janitor's closet. That is a direct reflection on how we are performing our work. I had a very large customer who judged the quality of our work by the condition of our janitor's closet. I had an agreement with him to do a once a month tour of his facility to see the level of quality we were performing. My promise to him was that I would not tell our crew when we were going to do the quality assurance tour. I kept my word and didn't let our staff know when I would be doing the tour. When we did the tour, the first place he checked was our janitor's closet. If it was in order, his comment went something like, "Ollek, it looks to me like your crew is doing a great job", and we would head to lunch. If he found dirty mop water, or a full brute from yesterday's trash, or a full vacuum bag, or a dirty floor machine, his comment was "looks to me like you are not keeping the facility up to the standard we agreed upon". Then we would walk the entire million square foot facility from one end to the other with no lunch. That didn't happen very often in the 20 years we maintained his facility but once was once too often. Boy, did my feet hurt when we got done with what was usually a 4 to 5 hour tour. No fun. He was a great customer though because he would also pick up the telephone and call me if he toured a section of the facility that was good, to let me know we were doing a great job. I really enjoyed working with him because whether he called to complain or to compliment I knew it was an accurate assessment of the quality.

So there you have 10 things that we do that affects the customer's impression of our company. Let me suggest you answer the following questions to see what additional items you can think of that affects your customer's impression of your company.

1. In addition to these 10 items, what other things does our company do that affects the customer's impression of our organization?

2. If any of the items listed above or that we have added are negative, what do we plan to do to turn them into a positive?

3. What training needs to take place in our company to make sure that EVERYONE understands the importance of good customer relations?

NOTE: Our company has produced a Customer Relations Training DVD available in both English and Spanish---www.consultantsincleaning.com.

LESSON 6

HANDLING COMPLAINTS

This aspect of being a good, effective supervisor is another extremely important one. Handling it incorrectly can mean losing the customer. Handling it properly will solidify your company's standing with that customer.

Let me list the important points in handling complaints. I want to emphasize that how you handle complaints is an important extension of good customer relations addressed in the previous lesson.

1. Respond NOW! The customer called now because he or she wants someone to address a particular issue NOW. Don't have messages go to your voice mail if you are in a position to answer the phone. Rapid response time tells your customer they are important and that helps keep customers.

2. Listen to the customer and get their complete explanation of the issue that is causing them concern etc. Don't make excuses. It never works. You see the reason they hired your company is because they didn't want to deal with the issues like employee absences, discipline, and the like. That's your job. Excuses only leaves the impression with the customer that you and/or your company has a lot of problems and are having difficulty handling them. Don't give them an additional opportunity to look to another company to provide their services.

3. Take notes. Having a notebook and pencil and writing down the customer's comments and concerns lets that customer know that they are important to you. Remember what I said earlier, treat each customer as if they are the only one you have.

4. Inspect the area of complaint or request WITH THE CUSTOMER to make sure you know exactly what is concerning them. By inspecting the area and taking notes of what transpired shows the customer you care AND it helps you remember what needs to be done when you get back to your office. Then proceed to handle the situation with your staff. In many starting and emerging companies, you may be that person who has to get the issue taken care of to the customer's satisfaction, so DO IT.

5. Tell the customer what you are going to do and when you are going to do it. Don't push the issue off onto another supervisor or the owners of your company. They probably have enough issues of their own.

6. Do what you said you would do for the customer and THEN FOLLOW UP WITH THAT CUSTOMER. Many good intentions are ruined with customers because we don't follow back up with them. They are left in the dark wondering if you fulfilled your promise which only leads to them doubting your company's interest in them as a customer.

For years my company had a 24 hour, 7 day a week call center where our customers could call from anywhere in USA where we operated and make a request or lodge a complaint or add additional services. Our call staff would log the call and then issue a work order to the appropriate district office for action, but here was probably the most important part of the entire procedure. The next day after the customer had called, our call center would call them back and ask if they were satisfied with the resolution of the issue etc. I cannot count how many times I received a positive comment from our customers appreciating the fact that we would call them back to assure satisfaction. In fact, I can remember two of my customers telling me that the issue was NOT resolved as requested but they were so impressed that someone called them back that they were okay with the fact they had to remind us a second time on the issue. Well, it may have been okay with them but it wasn't okay with me. You guessed it, I got personally involved to determine exactly what happened and took the corrective action immediately. By the way, I had a policy that if a customer called with a complaint that required immediate attention we would have someone on our staff take care of it and review the issue with the supervisor when they reported in for their shift. If a call came in for the same issue from the same customer a second time, I called the supervisor at home and had them go resolve the issue immediately. This usually stopped second time calls for that supervisor. We also would address additional training for the supervisor in question. A third time for the same thing with the same customer? I took them to lunch and bought theirs to go.

7. A good effective supervisor will, after following up with the customer, perform any necessary training with the staff to avoid any repeat of the issue. I mentioned in item 6 above, how I handled a supervisor who had a repeat issue and you will notice I mentioned additional training as an important part of the process. Well, it is just as important to conduct the additional training with the staff. Believe me, an efficient and effective supervisor will want to conduct the additional training necessary to avoid being called out when they just got to bed after a tough shift. Your company may choose not to follow the procedure we used but it worked for us.

As we close out this lesson on handling complaints, here are some suggestions,

1. Be sure you have IN WRITING your company policy on how to handle complaints.

2. Think of a customer complaint that you have had that wasn't handled well. What could you have done better?

3. What additional training do you need in order to be confident that you can handle any complaint situation that may arise?

LESSON 7

CONDUCTING DISCIPLINE

Maybe the first thing we should do in this lesson is to define discipline just as we defined supervision in lesson 1 so here we go,

DEFINITION OF DISCIPLINE—TRAINING TO FIX INCORRECT BEHAVIOR AND/OR CREATE BETTER SKILLS.

While some may feel that conducting discipline is "I gotcha", that is a definition that I believe belongs to the "olden" days. Look at the second part of the definition—create better skills. What that says is that while discipline can be an unpleasant task that has to be performed it can also be a positive opportunity to retrain an employee and help them improve their skills.

In all my years of being in business, the area of discipline is one area that I really hated to deal with and I don't think I am alone in that feeling. While I worked hard at the issue, as I look back, I realize there were a lot of mistakes made. Usually the mistakes I made were in taking too long to take the necessary disciplinary action. Don't think I am alone in this problem.

So that new and old supervisors can learn from my mistakes, I want to list in this lesson, eleven steps I believe are critical in having a workable, fair discipline system in your company.

Before we begin reviewing those steps though, I believe is critically important that you do the following two things,

1. Be sure you thoroughly know your company policies inside and out. Now would be a good time to pull out the company policy manual and review. Let me suggest you should have one with you at all times for a handy reference for any incident that may require discipline. Each company has to establish their own policies depending on the culture that has been established.

2. Be sure you know the state laws in addition to federal laws as they pertain to your position in the company. As part of this lesson that should be discussed in great detail.

STEP 1

Whenever possible, discipline should be carried out by the immediate supervisor. You are probably saying something like "I know that" but many times I find supervisors, especially newer ones, want to wait and let their superior handle the issue and sometimes in the case of a very severe issue that may be the case, but most issues can and should be handled by the immediate supervisor.

STEP 2

Get all the facts as accurately and as rapidly as possible. Please note, I said get all the facts, not opinions. When an issue that requires disciplinary action occurs, more often then not, the opinion of the supervisor and those that witnessed the incident will cloud the facts. If the person being disciplined is not particularly well liked or has maybe been difficult in the past, opinion many times gets in the way of the facts. Just remember, opinions don't count, facts do when conducting discipline.

Let me also mention that performing effective discipline is not sending them to the office the next day for them to "take care of it". The office doesn't know what happened, you do. It just leaves the employee with a feeling of no one knows what they are doing. Take it from someone who experienced it.

STEP 3

Discipline promptly. When a violation occurs it is imperative that action be taken immediately. The longer you wait the more the facts get clouded and opinion settles in. When you wait till later etc., people around you begin to think that the incident must not have been too serious or you would have taken action immediately. If you don't take action immediately it can also be construed by the fellow workers that it must be okay. You see, that is one of the major points about discipline. If you take action late or take no action at all, the work force construes that to mean that the behavior must be okay. Prompt discipline when needed is an absolute necessity.

STEP 4

Always discipline in private. This is an unpleasant task and should always be handled in private. There are times as well that you should have a witness present during the disciplinary discussions. Here I must defer to your individual company to instruct on the procedure to follow. Different states have different laws in addition to federal government laws and this relates back to my opening comments in this lesson of knowing what you company policy is and what the state and federal laws are in relation to the incident being addressed.

STEP 5

This step is many times one of the most difficult to keep in mind when having to conduct discipline. That is to always be FIRM, FAIR AND CONSISTENT. Most people have difficulty doing this step because most of the time it is a task that needs to be done with someone you have been working with on a regular basis. It is important to know what you company policies are and be able to enforce them in a firm manner. Remember, you must address only the situation you are reprimanding the worker for. You emotions cannot enter into the event. What was the violation, and how must it be handled in this particular case. You may or may not like the individual but this cannot have any bearing on what you must do. Being consistent is really important in that if you have established a particular penalty for the infraction, you must deal with it consistently with how you have dealt with it in the past. One very important factor here is to not "get in the weeds" with the individual. As we have stated before, you must do the discipline promptly, explain the violation and why it is a violation, state what you plan to do and get back to work. This may be a golden opportunity to do some additional training of the individual so a recurrence can be avoided in the future. Remember, one of the responsibilities of a good supervisor is to train their staff members so they become valuable assets to the organization. The cost of recruiting and bringing a new employee onto the payroll and training them for their job is upwards of $500 per person so unless the violation is one that requires immediate termination you should always attempt to keep the employee. Sometimes they just won't accept the consultation for improvement but a good supervisor will always make the effort to make them a better employee.

STEP 6

Step number 6 is to always consider the circumstances of the issue and the individual involved. Lest you think this presents the opportunity to favor one employee over another, let me give you a couple of examples of employees being late for work.

Employee number one comes to work 30 minutes late and your normal question would be to ask why he or she is late. The answer for this example is their car wouldn't start so you ask why it wouldn't start and they proceed to tell you the battery on their car was dead. So you ask if they got a new battery so they could come to work and they say "no, I haven't got the money for a battery". It just so happens yesterday was payday so you ask the obvious question of why didn't he or she have the money for a new battery? The explanation is that they decided to have a few beers with the gang last night after work and they spent their paycheck. You continue to ask the why question and then have to decide what action to take.

Employee number two also comes in 30 minutes late and you ask the same question, why? It so happens their spouse had a heart attach earlier that day and was taken by ambulance to the hospital and is in intensive care. "I know I was to call in 3 hours in advance but time just got away from me and I was worried about my spouse".

Now, would you handle each of these situations alike? They both showed up for work 30 minutes late but under entirely different circumstances.

My question to the second employee probably would be something like why are you here? You should be at the hospital with your spouse?

The first employee will require some sort of action depending on your company policies for arriving late for work but the second employee has, what I would consider, an understandable reason for being late and would receive no discipline.

That is what I mean when I say consider the circumstances and the individual. In fact, for the second employee you would want to get the details and send flowers or a card or something else appropriate.

One more thing to consider doing in each situation you are confronted with that may require some sort of disciplinary response. I had a policy to always ask "why" 5 times. Usually by the third or fourth why you get the REAL reason for the infraction. Then you make the decision of what action, if any, to take. Try it next time. You may be amazed at some of the answers you receive.

STEP 7

If you are confronted with a situation that you feel warrants immediate termination, it is always a good policy to discuss it with another supervisor or manager. Remember, we want to save people and try to retrain them in a positive manner so they become better employees for us but sometimes that just can't be done.

Sometimes the situation is such that we get too emotionally involved and discussing the issue with someone else as referred to above brings another opinion into the incident that has escaped your mind because of your total involvement in the matter.

STEP 8

DOCUMENT! DOCUMENT! DOCUMENT! I can not over emphasize the importance of this step in the discipline process. All of the work done in conducting necessary discipline can be completely negated if the proper paperwork is not done.

Whenever an employee consultation takes place a note or form should be placed in their file in case it is needed in the future. Many an unemployment case has been lost, even if the company was 100% correct, because there was no supporting documentation in the file.

Even if the infraction is a minor one, documentation showed be placed in the file, EVEN IF IT IS ONLY A VERBAL DISCUSSION.

My policy was to have the employee sign any documentation that occurred so we had a trail of what happened. Even if the employee refused to sign the consultation form or note, we would mark "over" at the bottom of the form, turn it over and write the words, "Employee refuses to sign this document" and then I would ask the employee to sign that they were refusing to sign. In this way you still have a signature that there was a discussion about the issue in question. It sounds strange but it does work and even then if the employee refuses to sign, you can sign and have documentation.

Even if the infraction is very minor, ALWAYS put some sort of documentation in their file. I have been to many unemployment hearings and can attest to the fact that documentation is the key to any hearing that takes place.

As an additional note, your company's state unemployment rate is determined by the amount of dollars paid to an employee collecting unemployment benefits that are charged to your company's account. Anytime the company has unemployment benefits charged to their account and has their rate increased that takes away from the profitability and ultimately dollars for more employee wages.

STEP 9

Always explain to the employee why the infraction is a problem. Each one stands on its own but it could be because it affects the safety of the whole crew, or in the case of excessive absences it should be explained how it affects the quality of work performed which can ultimately lose a customer and the jobs that go with the account.

STEP 10

Always remain calm and in control of the situation. I have witnessed supervisors getting into arguments with the erring employee only to compromise the entire situation. When you start arguing, you are "getting in the weeds" with them and YOU LOSE. Remain calm, discuss the situation, and don't let you emotions or personal feelings for the individual get in the way. As an effective supervisor you are to conduct the issue in a professional, calm, and confident manner. If you don't, the word will get around and you eventually lose control of the work force you are entrusted with supervising. This then affects your standing in the organization.

STEP 11

The final step in conducting discipline is that you FOLLOW UP WITH THE EMPLOYEE AND REESTABLISH POSITIVE CONTACT. Remember, the supervisor's job is to try and help the employee be of more value to the company. You conducted the discipline, took the action needed, and now the issue is hopefully resolved and should be put behind you so that everyone can again concentrate on satisfying the customer.

Here again it is important that you not let personal feelings or emotions continue to linger. You had an issue, you resolved it, and now let's "get back to work".

As a review to this lesson on discipline let's answer the following questions,

1. Take out a piece of paper and a pencil, close the book and list the 11 steps to take in conducting effective discipline.

2. After completing the list, see which ones you missed and review them again until you know all 11 by heart.

3. Determine which of the steps you need additional information or training in and then ask for help in where to get what you need. It is important in becoming an effective supervisor.

Our company has a training DVD on Discipline in both English and Spanish---www.consultantsincleaning.com.

Let me close this lesson with a quote by Gruenter and Whitaker,

"The culture of any organization is shaped by the worst behavior the leader is willing to tolerate".

LESSON 8

DEALING WITH DIFFERENT GENERATIONS AND CULTURES

We've covered a lot of ground on what goes into becoming an effective supervisor. Now it is time to look at an area that has really become important in that last few years and will become even more critical in the years to come and that is understanding the different generations and cultures that you have in your workforce. How you work with and understand these differences can and will make a huge difference in your success as a supervisor.

Let's discuss the different generations first. We basically have 6 different generations and each of them come with a different mindset about their job and life in general. So let's take a brief look at each one of them and see if you can identify the people in your area of responsibility.

Before I start listing the different traits let me mention that what I list is not my opinion. It is just the way the different generations view things. No opinion here or least not one that I will express in this book.

Let me also mention that I pulled the information that follows on these generation traits etc. from several different sources.

TRADITIONALISTS OR SILENT GENERATION

This is the group that was born generally before 1946. Some of the key people during this era were President Eisenhower, Adolf Hitler, Winston

Churchill and President Franklin Roosevelt. (Have you youngsters reading this heard of these world figures)?

Some of the traits that this group has are,

A. A strong sense of civic pride which means you vote at every election to make your feelings known.

B. Avoid debt, pay cash for everything. Many in this group grew up or their parents grew up in the great depression of the 1930's and have many memories of the hardships they endured.

C. Many didn't have refrigerators, TVs, or radios. Seeing an airplane in the sky was very rare, if at all.

D. Once you took a job you expected to be there for life. If you changed jobs you were considered a job hopper and there must be something terribly wrong with you.

E. There was no such thing as divorce. You married for life, good or bad.

F. Retirement? What's that? You took a job and worked it until you died or couldn't work anymore.

G. A very cautious generation. Study thoroughly before proceeding.

BABY BOOMERS

This group was born generally between the years of 1946 and 1964. Some of the key people during this era were the Kennedy family, Martin Luther King, and John Glenn.

Some of the traits of this generation are,

A. This was the rock and roll generation.

B. Referred to as the "me" generation. What's in it for me.

C. Saw the ushering in of the Civil Rights movement.

D. Lived and protested during the Viet Nam war.

E. The beginning of Women's lib.

F. The advent of Television.

G. Buy now and use credit to pay for it.

H. The wife started working outside the home so more amenities could be enjoyed by the family.

I. Divorce became accepted.

J. A pretty self centered generation. (Remember I said these are not my opinions but results of studies done).

This generation, at the time of this writing, has about 80 million people.

GENERATION X

This generation was born between the years 1965 and 1980. They grew up pretty street smart, often coming from split families. Some of the famous people in this generation are Bill Gates, Madonna and Michael Jackson. Some of the traits of this generation are,

A. Very entrepreneurial.

B. They have very little interest in big business and government.

C. Tend to be more self-centered.

D. Drugs really took hold while this generation was growing up.

E. Want what they want NOW and don't want to wait on it like the traditionalists did.

F. Very unimpressed with authority.

G. Mostly raised by a family that has both Mom and Dad working full time and many times in a family split by divorce.

H. Are not impressed by staying with one job for a lifetime. If the deal is better somewhere else, take it.

I. Usually are very heavily in debt prompted by their desire to have what they want now.

GENERATION Y (WHY)

This group was born between 1981 and 2000 and is much different than the traditionalists or baby boomers with characteristics such as,

A. Most ethnically diverse.

B. Very interested in a "green" world.

C. Question authority.

D. Are really tech wired and savvy.

E. Don't know about rotary phones, a time without a cell phones, or why the older folks don't want to use a computer.

F. They are a very smart, optimistic, and confident group.

G. Are into the "everybody wins" philosophy such as T-ball for kids where everybody wins.

H. Want to be team players but won't hesitate to switch jobs if they "feel" the new job will be a better social place to work.

I. Have never lived in a world without computers and have little patience for people who aren't proficient at using them.

J. Want information NOW.

K. They usually have been told by parents and teachers that they are a special generation and so they expect to be treated accordingly.

L. Prefer to work in teams.

M. They don't live to work like the older generation, they prefer to work to live.

N. They want to work with positive people.

O. They want to have a job that challenges them.

P. They want to work in a friendly environment.

Q. They want to be paid well.

By the way, this group at the time of this writing, make up over 100 million of the United States population.

GENERATION Z

This group was born around 2001 and soon will be entering the full time work force. They are a key work force at this time for the fast food industry. This group is many times referred to as the computer generation. Find what you need on the internet.

Some traits to note on this group are,

A. In 2006 the United States had a record number of births and nearly half of those born were Hispanic which greatly changes the dynamics of the upcoming work force.

B. Over half of this generation has a television in the room. Remember, the traditionalists probably didn't even have a TV.

C. They are a big economic spending group which means many retailers focus their advertising on them.

D. Most of them have their own cell phones.

E. They know what they want and how to get it.

F. Start using computers at the age of 3 or 4 and become very proficient quickly.

The list I have provided above in no way represents a complete picture of these generations and by now you have probably taken issue with some of the traits. That's okay, it is meant only as a snap shot picture. Can you add to each of the generations?

Think about it. As an effective supervisor you must manage all of these different personalities and philosophies. That is why we listed all of the points of discipline in the previous lesson because it is important that you deal with each of these generations in a manner that they understand what you are really saying.

Dealing with a 60 year old working in your area can take an entirely different twist than dealing with the 20 year old that has a completely different outlook on the world and the work place.

Think about some of the phrases and words used today by the younger generations and how the older generation might interpret the same thing.

For example, today's generation says you can buy anything you want on Ebay. The older generation says you could buy in the olden days anything from the Sears catalog.

GPS on your phone is how you find where you are going, right? The older generation used something unique called a map.

Today we can google earth for anywhere. The older generation used something called a globe.

Craig's list is used to advertise anything and everything today.

Craig's list to the older generation was that little black book Craig had that listed all his girlfriend's phone numbers.

Text is what everyone does today instead of calling. Text to the older generation is the passage in the Bible that the minister uses as his theme for the Sunday morning message (sermon).

It seems everyone today has a twitter account so they can tweet. To the older generation tweet meant Tweety bird on the Saturday morning cartoon show.

Today's generation uses facebook---the older generation used something called a yearbook.

Yahoo to the older generation is the outhouse in the yard for those that didn't have indoor plumbing.

Wikipedia is the easy way to find about anything you want these days. The older generation used the encyclopedia.

Remote is something used today for turning on the TV and other electronic devices. Remote to the older generation was that house way out in the sticks that was hard to get too--"You really live in a remote area".

Taking it even another step further, think about the computer we use every day and how traditionalists like myself have had to adjust our vocabulary. For instance,

We always thought a window was something you clean.

A program was a TV show.

The keyboard was the piano I took lessons on as a youngster. (Yes, I do play the piano---poorly).

A cursor was the local school bully.

An application was what we give to prospective employees.

A ram to me always was a cousin to the goat or today Dodge makes ram trucks. Probably not the same thing.

Meg was Bill's girlfriend when I was in school. Wonder whatever happened to her.

Gig was something musicians got or something we got as a part time job.

I always thought compressing was something you did to trash not to computer files.

Unzipping is normal on computer files today. When I was growing up if you unzipped, you probably ended up in jail.

Log on meant put more wood in the fireplace.

Now we paste files on our computers. I did pasting with glue.

A web was a spider's home.

My generation had the flu when they had a virus. Not so in today's computer world.

> Now, if the task of working with the different generations wasn't daunting enough, you also have the cultural differences to deal with. Many companies in the Building Service Contracting field now employ many groups of people that migrated here from Europe, Asia, and South of the United States border.

> To demonstrate some of the differences that occur, I want you to do an exercise that will help you understand this challenge. I want you to get a piece of paper and pencil and write down your definitions to the following words. Ready?

1. Lead
2. Boot
3. Record
4. Fire
5. Train
6. Diamond
7. Hike
8. Bad
9. Bonnett

Got it, okay let's look at each of these words.

LEAD—This can mean leading a group as a lead person on a crew. Or lead can also be lead such as "get the lead out".

But when training a group from, say Europe, this definition may mean the cord of a vacuum cleaner. I plugged the lead into the socket.

BOOT---This one seems simple enough but it can be construed as something you put on your feet. Some people also say that when they get terminated like "I got the boot".

Again, in some countries the boot is the trunk of the car. Quite different than something you put on your feet, isn't it?

RECORD---This can be record or reecord. Another one of those words that can be pronounced two ways. Do you have a police record or another way is my favorite singer has a new record out. Either way it can be confusing to someone from another country trying to learn how to communicate in the workplace.

FIRE---Did you say hot or burning? That would seem to be a logical definition for fire. Another way it has been defined, and especially by traditionalists and baby boomers is as another word for being terminated. "I was fired".

To demonstrate what I mean I want to relay a story that happened to a good friend of mine.

As a teenager he had a job as a grocery sacker and then taking the groceries to the car for the shopper.

One day as he was placing the groceries in the trunk (boot) of the car, the bag split open and the contents splattered all over the ground. Well, the customer was angry and immediately went back inside to discuss the matter with the store manager.

As a result of the customer's conversation, my friend was invited into the store manager's office and told he was being terminated. My friend said okay and just sat there. The manager asked him if he heard what he said. My friend said I heard you but don't understand what terminate means. The store manager put it another way, "You're fired". Now I understand my friend replied.

The story illustrates that we cannot take for granted everyone understands what we are saying. Not only is this a generational issue but a cultural issue. As an effective supervisor it is important that you make sure your staff understands exactly what you are saying and what you mean.

TRAIN---Most of the time the answer I get on this one is locomotive or choo choo. That is a logical definition but what about train as a definition for teaching our employees how to perform their jobs in an excellent manner. We have a training class coming up or I need to train you on this issue could be construed, especially by employees of a different nationality, to mean you are going to have a class on locomotives. Here in the United States not a lot of travel is done by train but in many foreign countries the train is the major source of transportation.

DIAMOND---This one usually brings answers like expensive, rock, or engaged. Being a baseball fan, the first thing that came to my mind was a baseball diamond. A long ways from an expensive rock isn't it? I should say my wife did not have the same definition that I did. She trended more toward an expensive rock.

I want to relay a true story that happened to me a few years back. I was asked to conduct a series of supervisor's workshops for a company that cleaned several 24/7 accounts. That in itself may not be especially unique except that their entire workforce was a non English speaking Eastern European staff. Through the use of an outstanding translator we got through 3 days of workshops and at all times of the day and night. First time I ever started a workshop at 2 in the morning.

Anyway, as we were doing this exercise on word definitions, I relayed that my definition was about baseball. No one in any of the sessions understood what I was talking about. You see, they came from a country where baseball was not played and it didn't mean a thing to them. Another word to the wise, always know your audience. I knew mine but wanted to test my theory of making sure everyone understands what we are talking about.

HIKE---This one usually brings answers like, a trail, journey, or football. Some participants replied that they were told by their spouse to "take a hike". Not sure if that was true but I am sure you have heard that phrase in some conversation somewhere.

Another definition, and one that I like is, "I got a hike in pay" which is another way of saying you got a raise.

BAD---This one can really cause confusion among workers with origins in other countries. When I was growing up bad meant something terrible had happened or that is a bad person or business is bad.

Today's younger generation has taught me that bad is good. Huh? Communicating with my grandchildren has taught me a lot.

Imagine communicating with a worker from a different culture and, you being a younger supervisor, and making a comment on their excellent work like "that's really bad". You know what you mean but if they don't know that bad means good, you can have a very sad, disappointed employee who thought they were doing a great job.

BONNET---This can have several definitions. It can mean a head covering that women wear or if you are in the carpet cleaning business it can mean surface cleaning a carpet, like I am going to bonnet clean the carpet. If someone is from some areas of Europe a bonnet is the hood of a car. Now that can really confuse someone if you don't explain it properly.

Hopefully in this lesson you have got at least a basic understanding of an effective supervisor's responsibility in understanding and dealing with generational and cultural differences in the workplace. Those differences will continue to evolve and create challenges for the supervisor but one that can be a great learning experience.

As a review to this lesson, answer the following questions,

1. What additional differences do I see in the generations that are not covered in this lesson? Take each generation individually. Remember, we said we only scratched the surface.

2. See how many additional definitions you can add to the ones we outlined in our exercise on what do these words mean to you.

3. Discuss some issues you may have had dealing with different generations and cultures and how you could have maybe had a better result.

4. Discuss successes you have had in dealing with them.

5. What action are you going to take to assure that you improve in these areas?

LESSON 9

THE EMPLOYEE TRAINING ISSUE

In the service, and other industries for that matter, no subject receives more discussion and less results than does training. In fact, we consider it so important we are devoting 2 lessons to the subject in this book.

Nearly every sales proposal I have seen in the contract cleaning and related industries will have a section on how the proposing company employs trained personnel—usually it turns out to be POORLY TRAINED personnel.

Whenever I conduct a workshop on this subject of training, one of the exercises I have the participants do is to list what effective training of the worker means to them and their company.

Let's list some of them that come to mind. Again, let me encourage you to add to the list.

- REDUCTION OF TURNOVER---At the rate of $500 plus per employee to advertise, orient, train and put someone on the payroll, it doesn't take a genius to determine that this benefit comes near the top of the list. Let me suggest you review the number of W-2s your company made last year and see what the dollars come to. The Building Service Contracting industry has an average turnover rate of about 350% per year so if you had 100 workers on the payroll and you are an "average" company, you made 450 W-2s. Let's see, $500 times 350 W-2s which is the excess over the 100 that you regularly employ comes to

$175,000. That's an enormous amount of money that could not be used for wages of the great, loyal, dedicated employees that come to work every day and do their job to satisfy the customer. That dollar amount will have you searching for some nausea pills. I know I needed them the first time I ran the numbers for my company before I started to take steps to reduce that turnover number.

- HELPS RETAIN EXISTING CUSTOMERS---Ever had a customer tell you when they canceled your service that the main reason for terminating was your high employee turnover? Most companies, if honest, will admit they have, at least once, been told that. So, factor in the sales cost you have in finding new prospects and then turning them into long term customers and you have another big number and big reason to provide a quality ongoing training program in your company.

- HELPS OBTAIN NEW CUSTOMERS---One of the frequent questions being asked today by prospective customers is "what's your turnover rate"? I have seen service companies eliminated from consideration through this process. I have also seen service contractors become extremely creative in how they determine their turnover rate and how they answer that question. I didn't know there were so many ways to determine turnover rates until I heard some companies trying to explain their number to a prospective customer. The fact is, you can use any method you want but when you get back to the office the number is still what it is.

- CREATES A SAFER WORKPLACE---You may not have thought of this one, but properly trained employees have fewer work related accidents and fewer accidents result in lower workers compensation premiums for the company which again creates more bottom line dollars for salaries.

Here again, many prospective customers are asking the qualifying question of prospective service providers, "What is your workers compensation modification rate"? Many prospects today will not allow you to present a proposal if your modification factor is over 1.00. We'll discuss this in greater detail in a later lesson.

I am aware of a Building Service Contractor that was the incumbent contractor on a very large facility and was eliminated from the proposal process for renewal of the contract because their factor was 1.01. Even though the contractor pleaded with the customer for an exception, the customer was so safety conscious that they would not allow a waiver and the contractor lost a major piece of business they had been servicing for several years. The customer was that intent on a safe working environment.

I know you are probably saying there must have been another reason and they just used this as an excuse to use another vendor. I don't think that was the case but even if they did, why give them an opportunity to use this excuse. Develop an ongoing effective training program and keep the premiums at a manageable level.

- LOWER LABOR COSTS---You, no doubt have heard it said why is there never enough time to do the job right the first time but always time to do it over. Well, with the proper training, there are fewer times the job has to be done over. Make sense? Not to mention when a customer has to call you to complain that the job was not done correctly, you have lost creditability with that customer which brings you one step closer to making them a "former customer".

- LOWER MATERIAL COSTS---This one goes hand in hand with the lowering of labor costs. If a worker is trained in the proper way of using materials needed for his or her job, it stands to reason that there is less waste and overall cost of supplies.

- LOWER EQUIPMENT REPAIR---I can recall, prior to having a systematic training program and an in house repair department, having telephone conversations with the company that repaired our equipment about the misuse our equipment was getting. There will always be those who don't care no matter how much training you give them and those are the ones you need to take to lunch and buy theirs to go. But most people

WANT to do the job right and use the equipment properly. Train them properly and your equipment repair costs and new equipment purchases WILL GO DOWN.

I remember at one of our quarterly supervisor's/management meetings, one of our key managers was explaining for the umpteenth time how to properly empty a vacuum bag. As he was going through the process, one of the participants asked, "Bill, how many times are we going to have to hear how to properly empty a vacuum bag"? "I will continue to repeat this process until we learn how to do it properly" was the reply. You see, Bill had taken the vacuum he was demonstrating the procedure on from the building where the questioning participant worked. We did not embarrass this person in front of his peers but did talk with him after the meeting that it was his vacuum that we were using and that it would be best if he listened more and talked less and then follow the correct procedures.

I can go on talking about this but I have probably hit on the major reasons for doing training that most impact the profitability of your company.

As a consultant I am sometimes asked by clients to attend presentations they are receiving from potential vendors. They are asking me to listen to the presentations with them and help determine if they should make a vendor change and if so, who might be the best choice. I always leave the choice up to the client but do try to offer constructive points about the presentations.

As best I can remember, every presentation I have listened to had a portion devoted to "trained personnel" of the aspiring service provider.

Inasmuch as training is an obsession with me, I would suggest to my clients that they ask these questions of the presenters,

A. We would like to have a checklist of your new employee orientation and training process.

B. Please provide us a schedule of your upcoming training events.

C. We would like to schedule a visit to tour your training facility and to meet your trainer(s).

Generally these are questions that provide some separation of the presenters. I listen carefully to the responses and then advise my clients as to which of the presenters MAY have stretched the "trained personnel" concept just a bit. Nevertheless, I do encourage my clients to follow through on the response. Sometimes they do, sometimes they don't.

How about your company? Do you provide genuine training or is yours a training program of "on the job" which means you really don't have a training program?

You may be asking yourself, self, why is Dick being so hard on everyone about training? Doesn't he understand that our people turn over so fast, so what's the use, they'll be gone before we can complete any kind of thorough training?

I can't resist talking a bit about the recruiting and hiring process. I am convinced if you believe that employees will leave quickly so there is no use in providing thorough training procedures, you are right. Employees sense if you are serious about providing them an opportunity or if you feel they are just a body to get a job done.

In my book, Finding, Training, and Keeping GREAT Service Employees 101 I devote a considerable amount of space to the difference between recruiting and hiring. You hire to just fill a slot, you recruit in order to provide employment opportunities for people and an chance for them to grow with your company.

Okay, so you employ mostly part time employees. So? I had part time employees that stayed for 15 to 20 years and I considered them an outstanding asset to our organization.

You never know, your part time employee, if trained and treated with respect and sincerity may just want to join you full time at some point in time.

Let me suggest that if every company had a detailed, professional training program for all levels of the company AND a policy of recruiting rather than just hiring, the employees may just stay longer. Remember the reason we gave earlier in this lesson for having an organized training program.

Talking about turnover, I once visited with a restaurant mogul who had over 300 fast food locations under his direction and we were discussing the perils of turnover in the service business. As I was explaining my 80% turnover rate at the time, he explained to me that his average line worker lasted on the job for 8 days—8 DAYS. Now that's turnover. I believe he needed a training program or at least a better one.

One of the things that can make a systematic training program a challenge in the real world are the things we discussed in the previous lesson. We need to understand how to communicate with different cultures in our workforce as well as the different generations.

SO HOW DO WE TRAIN?

After spending my entire adult life training employees and visiting countless other companies who are trying to reduce their employee turnover and improve customer retention, I am convinced that for many, it isn't that they don't want to, but it is they don't understand the difference between training adults and training children. Oh yes, there are those who espouse the theory of why train, they will leave you anyway, but I continue to believe that most organizations want to do the right thing.

I have an Ollekism:

"It is better to train your people and have them leave then to not train them and have them stay".

Think about it. Wouldn't it be easier on all of us if the world we work in and the career we have chosen was full of qualified, well trained, GREAT employees? As an effective supervisor, your job is maybe not to train the world but how about making sure everyone that is your responsibility has and is getting first class training? If you train and treat them well, chances are they won't leave and not only is the job being done well, your company's turnover rate is dramatically reduced.

Even if they do leave, you have greatly improved the industry and who knows, they may come back to you once they find the competitor that offered them the moon really doesn't have anything to offer. So you are ahead either way.

So, let's examine this whole idea of training adults vs. training children.

First off, I think you will agree that you can order or mandate your adult employees into a training class but you can't force them to learn. Agreed? The fact is adults learn much differently than do children. I believe if you ask training professionals they will readily agree with me. While there are several theories about why adults learn differently than children, there are several reasons we know for sure. Adults have an entirely different motivation concerning learning and they filter information through a different mindset than do children.

I think it is important as a supervisor that you know and have a basic understanding of how adults learn as you think and talk about training the staff for which you have the responsibility.

Most employees experience with training is limited to what they were exposed to as children, sitting in a classroom listening to the teacher explain the subject of the hour. If you try to approach training that way in your organization, I submit to you that your training will FAIL. Bold words but I truly believe them.

"MOTIVATION TO LEARN"

So how can you motivate your potential super employees to learn? Sometimes that can seem like an impossible task when you are trying to teach someone to clean a toilet. There are several important facts we need to know about motivating adults to learn:

1. Adult learners can be motivated by appealing to their personal growth and wealth---in order to motivate adults to learn, you must tell them the "WIIFM"---What's in it for me"? They need to know the reason for taking the time and effort to learn something. You're an adult.

Aren't you maybe wondering the same thing? Do you have aspirations of moving up the company ladder and if you are a company owner reading this, wouldn't it be nice to develop a staff of effective, efficient, trained individuals so you didn't have to do it all? Do I have your attention?

2. Personal recognition can also be a powerful motivation to learn. It is a known fact that many people in the service industry suffer from low self esteem and confidence. The prospect of learning a new skill or improving on one they already have can offer a boost to that low self esteem. Supervisor, help build and improve your staff. You'll all benefit from it.

"CHILDREN VS. ADULTS IN LEARNING"

Let's review some of the differences in learning between children and adults. The differences are substantial and as I stated earlier, it is important that you know the differences so you will have success in your training process.

CHILDREN rely on others to decide what is important to learn. They go to school every day and the teacher has a lesson plan laid out for them that they are expected to learn and are tested on their comprehension of the material.

ADULTS on the other hand, decide for themselves what is important to learn. For example, you probably decided to buy and read this book on your own if you are an owner. Supervisors, on the other hand, are probably being told to read it (so you better read it or you'll have to go to time out). You may have been told to read it but no one can control IF you read it. You are in control. But, that also means your chances for advancement may take a hit.

CHILDREN accept information being presented in class at face value. If the teacher says there are 24 crayons in the box, the child believes it because they trust what the teacher says.

ADULTS will do what? They will want to count the crayons because they remember years ago buying some and being shorted two crayons in the box. That experience taught them to be cautious as to what people tell them. Fast forwarding to the current time, it is really an important issue. We are so inundated with falsehoods, internet hacking, and identity theft that most people just don't believe anything or anyone. This can make your job of effective supervision and training more difficult BUT it can also make it more rewarding if you will follow the steps to making training more exciting.

CHILDREN are told and expect that what they are learning will be useful to them in the long term. They are led to believe that the education they are getting now will result in a better paying job or career in the long run. If college students didn't believe that why would they take on such massive student loans to get an education?

ADULTS on the other hand, expect that what they are learning to be useful to them IMMEDIATELY. They expect to take what they are learning in the training session to be useful NOW, not 5 years from now.

CHILDREN have little or no experience to draw from---they have relatively "clean slates". They still believe everything they are told (scary). Think back to your childhood. Your parents and teachers were your source of information. With the internet, facebook, instagram, linkedin and how ever many others have sprung up since this writing, there are countless ways to get useful as well as incorrect information. They have a lot of sources to draw from and are still not really old and wise enough to separate truth from fiction.

ADULTS, on the other hand have much past experience upon which to draw. They have had time to form opinions and viewpoints which many times differ dramatically from the very people they were relying on for information in their youth. I know many of my viewpoints have changed since I was a child. I don't necessarily disagree with what I was told, I just have more facts on which to form an opinion. It is important to remember that the employees you are wanting to train also have had the opportunity to learn new and different views on a variety of the subjects you may be trying to teach them.

Richard D. Ollek, CBSE, RGC

Recognizing the differences will make a huge impact on whether your training is successful. As a successful, effective supervisor it is important that you keep these differences embedded in your mind in order to execute the positive training needed with your staff.

Please remember this--"People don't care about how much you know until they know how much you care". Keep this as a focus on your training and you overall supervisory responsibilities and your chance at success will be multiplied many times over.

In the next lesson we will be addressing more ways to conduct successful training, but before going on please answer and discuss the following questions,

1. What are the major benefits of having an effective training program that we outlined in this lesson?

2. What additional benefits can you think of for your company other than those listed?

3. List some changes you should consider in your training program now that we have confirmed that children and adults learn differently? What are you going to change NOW?

4. Can you describe a training session you conducted that may not have gone as you wanted it to? What could you have done differently to make it more effective?

LESSON 10

CREATING EFFECTIVE TRAINING

In this lesson we want to continue with the subject of assuring that all of the people that you are responsible for as an effective supervisor can learn and have fun doing it.

In the previous lesson we spent time discussing the difference between children and adults in how they learn but it is also very important to understand how adults remember information.

We have different levels of retention of information depending on how we learn something. The more of our senses we involve in the learning process, the better chance that we will remember. For example we remember:

- 10% of what we read

- 20% of what we hear

- 30% of what we see

- 50% of what we see and hear

- 80% of what we say

- 90% of what we say AS we do

This may help to explain why those training programs that tell employees to read something (this book excepted), and watch a video and then sending them to the field don't usually succeed. At best the employee has a chance of retaining 20%. Not good!

Here are some of my suggestions for creating effective training in your organization.

"LET THE LEARNER PARTICIPATE"

I always suggest a company purchase some round tables for their training workshops as it is important to have the participants working on group exercises. You may not be able to take advantage of this suggestion if you are training one a day but when you bring all your people back in for the 2 time yearly refresher course (with pay), the round tables will be a valuable asset in the learning process.

Roundtables provide the opportunity for people to express themselves with a small group and learn from that small group. Let's face it, some people just are not comfortable speaking in front of a large group but they will talk with 4 or 5 at the same table. Give them that learning opportunity whenever possible. They will also gain confidence so someday they may be able to speak in front of the entire group. I know it happened to me. My senior trainer had her knees knocking when talking in front of 6 people but became a seasoned trainer pacing around the room doing an outstanding job without notes. She was a real winner.

"MAKE THE TRAINING FUN"

I found that, for the most part, the more fun we can have during the learning process, the more we learn. For example, don't be afraid to tell a joke on yourself. As a supervisor or even before you became a supervisor, did you make some silly mistake. I know I did. I remember trying to conduct a class on carpet spotting and finally one of my senior supervisors said to me, "Dick, go sit down, I'll show them how to do it right". She was good and the group got a good laugh at the expense of the boss.

A word to the wise here for all supervisors. You don't know everything and your employees will respect you more for telling them you don't know but you'll find out. Then FIND OUT.

Some people I have worked with have taken the approach that because they are supervisors or managers they can't let the staff find out they may not know something. They will respect you more for saying "I don't know but I'll find out", than if they find out you lied to them, and they WILL find out.

"OFFER PRIZES FOR CORRECT ANSWERS"

One way I found very effective was to make up several envelopes with different bills like $5, $10, $20 and gift certificates to food stores, fast food restaurants etc. You will be amazed at how spending a few dollars on a few prizes will get participation in a training class. Have them draw an envelope for a great answer etc. Don't hand it to them or it may appear you are determining who gets what prize.

By the way, I have found that people who are bashful or don't want to speak up in a group setting will all of a sudden find that inner self when you start awarding cash prizes or gift certificates. You soon find attendees asking after every correct answer (or even before) if it qualifies for a prize. The participation is what speeds along the learning process.

"USE THE EXPERIENCES OF THE LEARNER"

An excellent exercise to use is the one I had you complete at the beginning of lesson 5. Don't remember it? Shame on you. Now is a good time to review it, we'll wait.

By using this method of learning you have used the process of letting the learner participate. See how each of these different ways of learning can build on each other?

"REPEAT THE IMPORTANT PARTS OF
THE TRAINING AT LEAST 6 TIMES

Always empty the vacuum bag after each use
Always empty the vacuum bag after each use
Always empty the vacuum bag after each use
Always empty the vacuum bag after each use
Always empty the vacuum bag after each use

Always empty the vacuum bag after each use

That's not exactly what I had in mind when I said repeat the important parts of the training at least 6 times. The point I am making is that during the training process you want to be sure that an important part is covered at least 6 times. You will want to explain the entire process of vacuuming and work into the training the importance of emptying the bag.

Then, when you have the employee explain AND SHOW you the process of correct vacuum care you will want to make sure they, and you, cover the process of emptying the vacuum bag every time upon completion of their shift.

If it hasn't been covered up to now, let me list the main reasons employees leave a job in the service industry.

1. Nobody told them what to do.

2. Nobody ever compliments them on a job well done.

3. They feel there is no room for advancement.

4. Nobody provided them with training on do the job correctly and efficiently.

5. No benefits.

Now, let me provide statistics of a survey done as to why people stay on the job.

What follows are survey results released in 2015 from Gallup Organization Q12 meta-analysis work measuring employee engagement and then provided to BSCAI members via the weekly Affinity HR Group in their newsletter. The results listed the 12 aspects of work that highly productive and engaged workers cite as motivating them on the job:

1. I know what's expected of me.

2. I have the materials and equipment I need to do my work right.

3. At work, I have the opportunity to do what I do best every day.

4. In the last 7 days I have received recognition or praise for doing good work.

5. My supervisor or someone at work seems to care about me as a person.

6. There is someone at work who encourages my development.

7. At work, my opinions seem to count.

8. The mission or purpose of my organization makes me feel my job is important.

9. My associates or fellow employees are committed to doing good quality work.

10. I have a best friend at work.

11. In the last 6 months, someone at work has talked to me about my progress.

12. This last year, I have had opportunities to learn and grow.

Claudia St. John, the president of Affinity HR Group does an outstanding job of providing helpful Human Resource information to the BSCAI membership and I don't miss a week of reading her newsletter. I know it has been very helpful to me.

Did you notice one thing missing from both of the lists? Not one mention of money in either of the survey results.

You have probably heard some or all of these reasons before and if you have attended one of my workshops you have heard most of these examples many times---maybe 6 times.

As an effective supervisor it is incumbent on you to address as many of these reasons and work at making sure that you keep your employees on the payroll if at all possible.

How does your company stack up?

"LET THE LEARNER APPLY WHAT THEY HAVE LEARNED"

If you recall, we said earlier in this lesson that 90% of what we remember is saying it AS WE ARE DOING IT. So, when you are proceeding through the training process it is extremely important that the participant DO what you have been training.

To use the vacuuming example referred to at the beginning of this lesson, the participant should be given the opportunity to teach back to you the operation and care of a vacuum. If they can't, we repeat the training until they can. Here is where repeating the process 6 times comes to the forefront. Maybe you need 8 times but don't assume because you have gone over it several times that they understand the process. Remember, IF THE LEARNER HASN'T LEARNED, THE TEACHER HASN'T TAUGHT. Keep pressing forward until you are confident they are performing the task to the standards your company has established.

Remember the process is one of we tell them how, we show them how, and they show us how. Once that process is standard in your organization, training, educating AND LEARNING will take place. The by-product of what I am talking about is that TURNOVER WILL GO DOWN.

"VARY THE DELIVERY PROCESS"

Another way for you to be an effective supervisor is to employ a variety of teaching methods. Some examples are,

A. Video, CD, DVD

B. Visual demonstration

C. Group exercises

D. Role playing

E. Guest presenters such as a distributor or manufacturer

F. Wall charts and graphs

G. Current experienced employees that do the tasks correctly

All of these are effective ways to get the point across. In our workshops we use a variety of methods in every session. I firmly believe it helps keep everyone's interest in what we are trying to accomplish.

One additional key to the training program is to have an ongoing refresher program. What in the world does that mean?

We required every employee to attend a paid refresher course every 6 months. We gave them several options of dates to attend but always made it mandatory for them to attend. They were taken through the new employee orientation as a refresher and introduced to any new products or equipment we were planning to implement into the system.

The fact is we all get into bad habits. We can have the best intentions but sometimes we just fall into a poor routine of doing a normal job. This mandatory refresher training every 6 months helps everyone to get back on track. Amazing the bad habits that are picked up in the field on some very simple tasks.

While I am on the subject of training, one valuable training process we had was a quarterly supervisor's/management workshop for existing supervisors and future stars for the company. These sessions relied heavily on the supervisors and managers for input AND presentations. It was a great way for them to gain additional training and presentation skills. Try it, you'll like it.

You may recall that we discussed in previous lessons how an effective supervisor needs to learn how to deal with the different generations and cultures in their area of responsibility. That means you also have to be able to conduct training sessions that focus on those generations and cultures. So, what are some of those ways? We mentioned some of them earlier in this lesson but let's go into a bit more detail here.

1. Create your own in house video training lessons. With the decreasing cost of owning video equipment, how about creating several 5 to 10 minute videos on such topics as

    a. vacuuming
    b. restroom cleaning
    c. proper trash dumping
    d. hard floor burnishing
    e. proper mopping techniques
    f. maintaining a clean custodial closet
    g. proper mixing of chemicals

    You can make movie stars out of some of your staff that perform the tasks in the prescribed way and then use them in the field or in the training center for learning the correct procedures. With the advancement of technology, doing follow up training in the field is really much easier than it was in the past. Use the tools you have and continue to reinforce your training.

2. If you don's want to invest in the video process create audio tapes that you can use in several ways. Most of the timekeeping systems in the marketplace today have messaging capabilities where an employee cannot clock in until that they listened to a message. Use this as an opportunity to teach.

    You can also post short videos on YouTube. Offer prizes for those that can identify a winning number that you post along with their required employee number.

3. Put short videos on the supervisor's cell phone so when a training issue arises, it can be dealt with right there. Great what we can do with our phones these days. More on the way.

4. You can also produce weekly pod casts for all to listen to or view about any subject you wish to address. This dove tails with number 3 but allows you to bring messages other than training. This is probably a good place to mention that we have a variety of FREE blogs and podcasts on our web sites for you to review.

5. Use short webinars for specific subjects and have the specified individuals attend. Pay them for attending.

6. One benefit some progressive distributors are now offering is creating an entire library of videos on just about every subject you can imagine about the industry that are produced by them and the manufacturers. They then lease tablets to the contractor for their supervisors so anytime there is a training issue that needs to be addressed they can access the distributor's library and get the information. This is an exciting advancement by some distributors. It's a great selling tool for the distributor and a wonderful training tool for the service provider. If you aren't already using a tool like this, ask your distributor if they have it available and if not, suggest it as a value added service for them to provide.

There are more and more ways being developed every day to provide better training methods to help reduce turnover. As an effective supervisor you have the responsibility to keep alert to new and better ways to train those valuable employees.

Always keep in mind the different age groups and cultural groups you have and strive to bring training to them in a way that best gets the message across to that group.

Remember, giving a 2 hour boring lecture, or just showing a video with no audience participation, or providing a session where you say "thou shalt not do this or thou shalt not do that will lose your employees in a heartbeat. Keep the training fun, full, upbeat, and positive.

As you review this lesson answer the following questions,

1. What are the most effective ways we remember things?

2. What are the most effective ways to conduct a training class with a group?

3. What steps do you as an effective supervisor need to take to improve the training in your area of responsibility and your company?

4. Which of the aspects of keeping employees engaged with your organization referred to in this lesson do you have? Should you be working harder at some of them to strengthen your company?

5. When and how do you plan to improve the training in your company?

LESSON 11

DEALING WITH BUDGETS

You may recall in lesson 1 we gave our real definition of supervision which really is a two part definition.

First, you must satisfy the customer so that you retain them and increase their satisfaction with your organization.

Second, an effective supervisor has the responsibility to bring all accounts in their area in on budget so the company produces the profit that was forecast for each account and therein lies the subject for this lesson.

There are several ways that companies keep track of the budgets on each account,

1. Don't track it but wait for the end of the month profit and loss statement to be completed and then wonder what in the world happened. This is not a recommended system but one followed by many organizations and can lead to their early demise.

2. Give the supervisor an hourly budget per night per account and ask them to stay on budget. This system usually gives very little latitude to the supervisor to financially reward the employees doing the best job.

3. With this procedure the supervisor is given a dollar budget for each account and gives the supervisor the leeway to recommend upward wage adjustments for the best performing employees.

In addition, with this method, the supervisor also can suggest hour adjustments to the account reducing hours if the work can satisfy the customer in less time spent or recommending increased hours if need be. You will notice I said the effective supervisor can suggest budget changes. I ALWAYS recommend that no changes in budgets, up or down, be made until a full discussion takes place with the supervisor's superiors.

I am sure there are probably other ways some companies and their supervisors deal with individual budgets but these three seem to be the ones most often utilized.

With today's modern technology an effective supervisor has many tools at their disposal such as telephone timekeeping, over and under reports, or hours comparison reports each day which tells which accounts were over budget or under budget the previous day.

It was my policy to review these each day by area and then have a conversation with the supervisor on any account that was over by 10% or under by 10% the previous day. An effective supervisor will know the answer as to why the deviation from budget occurred.

It was also my policy, in the case of an overage to require the supervisor get the hours back over no more than three days. After all, the account was sold on the premise of the budgeted hours and that is the amount of money the company has to spend. If the overage was due to additional requested work, an invoice needed to be generated. If the overage was due to correcting poor work, the requirement of getting on budget in three days stayed. The effective supervisor will do training or discipline to correct the deficiency within the allotted budget requirement.

If the account was under budget, it needed to be corrected that day because it could mean that we did not give the customer the service he or she paid for and was expecting.

In addition, if inspections are done as a good effective supervisor will do, deficient service should be noted and corrected immediately. I know this may sound negative but our lessons in this book are on helping supervisors become more effective and these are some helpful hints to do just that.

To help us better understand this whole budget issue, I want to spend just a few moments talking about "wasted time". Do you know how much five minutes a day wasted can cost your organization? Five minutes doesn't seem like much and studies have shown that most employees, good and not so good, waste much more than that, but let's just look at what 5 minutes can add up to.

Let's say as a supervisor you have 10 employees that you are ultimately responsible for. For the purposes of this discussion let's assume you are paying them each $10 per hour. Using this example, you will lose $2,520 per year. That's if they only waste 5 minutes per day.

I remember giving a presentation at a Building Service Contractors Association International convention a few years ago and I gave several examples of wasted time similar to the example above. After the session I had a contractor approach me with the words, "Your presentation made me sick". Well, that was a disconcerting evaluation of my presentation. He proceeded to explain that the presentation was great but that he had about 2,000 employees and was averaging about $12 per hour and he did the math and realized he was wasting about $604,000 per year--- that's if they only wasted 5 minutes each day, five days a week.

On the next page we have included a chart that shows what 5 minutes wasted per day costs. Let me suggest you take a few minutes and review the information and see where you fall.

"It's Only 5 Minutes"

What Only 5 Minutes Lost Each Day Costs In Annual Labor Dollars.

Hourly Rate	Employees								
	5	10	25	50	100	250	500	1,000	2,000
$ 8.00 ($ 9.60)	$ 1,008.00	$ 2,016.00	$ 5,040.00	$ 10,080.00	$ 20,160.00	$ 50,400.00	$ 100,800.00	$ 201,600.00	$ 403,200.00
$ 9.00 ($ 10.80)	$ 1,134.00	$ 2,268.00	$ 5,670.00	$ 11,340.00	$ 22,680.00	$ 56,700.00	$ 113,400.00	$ 226,800.00	$ 453,600.00
$ 10.00 ($12.00)	$ 1,260.00	$ 2,520.00	$ 6,300.00	$ 12,600.00	$ 25,200.00	$ 63,000.00	$ 126,000.00	$ 252,000.00	$ 504,000.00
$ 11.00 ($13.20)	$ 1,386.00	$ 2,772.00	$ 6,930.00	$ 13,860.00	$ 27,720.00	$ 69,300.00	$ 138,600.00	$ 277,200.00	$ 554,400.00
$ 12.00 ($ 14.40)	$ 1,512.00	$ 3,024.00	$ 7,560.00	$ 15,120.00	$ 30,240.00	$ 75,600.00	$ 151,200.00	$ 302,400.00	$ 604,800.00
$ 15.00 ($18.00)	$ 1,890.00	$ 3,780.00	$ 9,450.00	$ 18,900.00	$ 37,800.00	$ 94,500.00	$ 189,000.00	$ 378,000.00	$ 756,000.00

➢ Based on 254 working days per year and 20% for overhead cost to include F.I.C.A., Federal and State Unemployment taxes, and Workers Compensation insurance.

So, what's your number? Surprised? The real issue is that most people waste much more than 5 minutes on their job each day. Do you?

Let me give you an example that happened to me a few years ago. We had an account that was budgeted at 16 hours per night, Monday through Friday on which we used four people, four hours each per night.

While the account was running reasonably well, it seemed like almost every day we were plagued by "little" things such as the staircases not being swept, a lone towel dispenser not being filled etc. I worked with the crew trying to correct the situations but the issues continued and I could tell the customer was becoming frustrated with our inability to solve the "little" things that created havoc with the tenants.

My crew pleaded with me to just give them 15 minutes each per shift and the problems would be solved. In their words they just could not get all the work done in the 4 hours allotted to each person.

Finally I relented and asked the customer for some time to discuss the need for more time. She told me that she was about to leave for the day as it was close to 5 PM but she would wait for me so we could discuss the issue.

Well, after sweating tears and blood for an hour, my customer agreed to the additional dollars and I left excited and proud of the selling job I had accomplished on this valuable account.

The time was 6:20 PM and I decided to go to the lower level break area and reward myself with a soda and when I walked into the room, there was all 4 of my crew members sitting and visiting. Let's see, twenty minutes times four people equates to 80 minutes. Eighty minutes times 5 days per week times 260 times per year—oh well I was to ill (and angry) to do the math.

I explained to the crew that I had just had a battle getting them 15 additional minutes per shift per person and here I find them sitting in the break area 20 minutes after their shift was to begin. Fortunately for all of us the customer did not follow me into the break room. The explanation from the group was "this is the first time we have ever done this". What do you think? Was it the first time? Do you think I believed them? I learned a valuable lesson here and hopefully it helps you in your job of being an effective supervisor.

I made it a habit to review the 5 minute chart every few months with our supervisors just to remind them to be alert about wasted time. It wasn't used to beat them over the head but rather to just give them a reminder of the money that can be lost if we don't keep abreast of our budgets in each account.

Another area that can be very helpful in assuring efficient budgets in every account is to do a two times yearly retuning. By this I mean going through with a check list to make sure everything is in order and the account budgeted hours and dollars are adjusted to what is actually needed.

On the pages that follow is a sample account retuning worksheet that may be helpful. You, no doubt, will need to edit it to conform to the items you want to audit in your accounts but the one shown was the one we used for most of our accounts.

ACCOUNT RETUNING WORKSHEET

DISTRICT _____ ACCT. NAME _____

AREA _____ ACCT. # _____

SUB AREA _____ DATE COMPLETED _____

COMPLETED BY _____

1. Current employment policies & procedures handbook? ☐ Yes ☐ No
   Located _____

2. Current supervisors handbook? ☐ Yes ☐ No
   Located _____

3. Current employee job descriptions for all employees? ☐ Yes ☐ No
   Located _____

4. Current specifications for building dated _____
   Located _____

5. Instructions for using telephone timekeeping system? ☐ Yes
   ☐ No
   Located _____

6. Current Material Safety Data Sheets? ☐ Yes ☐ No
   Located _____

7. Current company and customer emergency telephone numbers posted in closet?
   ☐ Yes ☐ No

8. Current emergency procedures for injuries posted? ☐ Yes ☐ No

9. **ALL** keys current, properly marked and secured. All **old** keys properly disposed
   of? ☐ Yes ☐ No

10. All equipment neat, clean, and safely working? Cords good, switches working,
    backpack filters clean, paper bags empty, blocks in good working order?
    ☐ Yes ☐ No

11. All chemicals properly labeled, including all spray bottles? ☐ Yes ☐ No

ACCOUNT RETUNING WORKSHEET
(Page 2)

12. Proper number and sizes of safety belts, safety glasses, rubber gloves, wet floor signs, etc.?

           ☐ Yes   ☐ No

13. Supply closet neat, clean, and in proper order?   ☐ Yes   ☐ No

14. All excess equipment is being returned. I am returning _____

_____

_____

15. All excess supplies are being returned. I am returning _____

_____

_____

16. Other comments, suggestions _____

_____

_____

17. Currently my labor hours budget is:

SUN	MON	TUE	WED	THU	FRI	SAT

Effective _____, my labor hours budget should be:

SUN	MON	TUE	WED	THU	FRI	SAT

I have completed the retuning process this date _____

Site Supervisor _____

Area Supervisor/Manager _____

District/Operations Manager _____

You will notice there are items on the sheet that don't pertain to hour budgets etc. such as having an employee policy manual in each account and MSD sheets in each account and posting emergency phone numbers for both the customer and your company.

One thing you will notice is we ask the question if the current specifications are posted. It is very important that the specifications posted have a date no older than one year. Even if there are no changes, post a new one with the current date.

I have seen several job specifications in closets that date back YEARS. This just does not present a company that is paying attention to details.

Many times we found excess supplies in the building and were able to return them to the warehouse. Several pieces of equipment also found their way back. Ahh, that's what happened to that floor machine.

Help stay on budget, do the retuning process and you just might find some labor dollars that can be used for additional wages for the staff or you may even find the 5 minutes that have been wasted in the account.

This lesson brings to the forefront the trait that we discussed in lesson 3 of having a basic understanding of math.

In addition, with all the computer technology available today, it is easy to put the form on your computer and conduct the retuning by just typing in the answers etc.---another trait needed by an effective supervisor.

We have just scratched the surface in this lesson on budgets but I can assure you that today's effective supervisor must have an understanding of the dollars connected to providing the customer satisfaction needed to keep happy customers. Keep up to date, embrace new technology, use it to help your company, and you will become a very effective supervisor.

As you review this lesson, here are some questions to answer,

1. How can I become better at managing the budgets of the accounts that I supervise?

2. Where can I get this knowledge and who can help me get it?

3. Which of my accounts need my attention right now to get back into budget?

4. When do I plan to retune all of my accounts?

5. What technology will help me better manage my area?

LESSON 12

THE IMPORTANCE OF SAFETY

After 50 plus years in business, one thing I have witnessed in the business world, as it relates to safety, is that most companies fall into one of three categories in regards to their commitment to safety.

Category 1 are those companies that only provide lip service to the issue. They mention it here and there at a company meeting but that is about as far as the commitment goes although they will tell you differently.

Category 2 are those companies that will conduct a session whenever there is a company training session and they may even offer prizes to different areas or divisions that have the lowest number of work related injuries.

Category 3 is that company that understands the important part safety plays in the well being of the organization and continues to work diligently at preserving a safe work environment for their valuable employees. They also understand the financial benefits of a safe work place and the repercussions of not addressing safety.

So, being truthful, which category does you company identify with?

Let's discuss how safety, good or bad, can affect an organization.

Richard D. Ollek, CBSE, RGC

"THE EMPLOYEE"

When the employee suffers a work related injury, it affects not only them but their entire family. If they have to be off work for any period of time it can really be devastating.

Oh, I know, workers compensation will pay a weekly amount after a certain waiting period but it doesn't equal their pay stub.

In addition, the service industry employs a large number of part time workers. In fact, the building service contracting and fast food industry employ huge numbers of part time workers. Now what does that all mean?

If a worker is injured on their part time job and have to be off work for a period of time it can also mean that are unable to work their full time job. Their full time employer has no obligation to provide compensation because the injury did not occur while working for them. The hardship just multiplied itself.

Oh, I know, there are people who will fake an injury, but I am of the opinion that most people want to work and want to do a good job for their employer and their family and are not inclined to fake an injury.

"THE SUPERVISOR"

Now let's look at some of the ways the supervisor is affected in the event of an on the job injury of a worker in their area.

Let's assume for the moment that the injury is not life threatening and that the worker will not have to be off work for any length of time. The injury occurs but as stated in a previous lesson, my recommendation is that the supervisor TAKE the injured employee to a predetermined medical facility for treatment.

I also recommend that the facility conduct a drug test to determine if drugs could have played a part in the employee's ability to perform their work thus causing the accident. Remember to check Federal, State, and Local laws to see if that can be done in your area. At the time of this writing, many social law changes are taking place throughout the USA, so be sure you can perform this test legally in your area.

While at the medical provider with your injured employee is a great time to complete the paperwork that is required. Most states require a written report be filed within a certain number of hours after the incident. Be familiar with the laws in your state.

Why do I recommend you complete the paperwork while at the hospital or doctor's office? Well, have you ever been to a hospital emergency room and got right in for treatment? First the paperwork, then the wait, then escorted to the treatment room, then more waiting etc. etc.

While the effective supervisor is waiting is the best time because the facts of the incident are fresh in their mind. The longer one waits, the more distorted the facts become. Soon they become, "I think this is what happened".

Now let's address another way that injuries affect the supervisor. While the supervisor is occupied with medical issues, are we confident that everything is going well in the area? How about the building where the employee was injured? Who now is doing their work? Will the employees leave at their appointed time even though not all the work may be completed? What about the other buildings the supervisor was going to visit that shift? By spending hours in an emergency room or clinic, what tasks won't get done today that had to be accomplished? What about that new employee that just started today and is confused and waiting for direction? Will they stay and wait or will they put the keys in the closet and tell you what you can do with your job?

Let's now go one step further. Assume the injured employee is required to be off work for a period of time. Now comes the challenge of how do we get the work done?

The effective supervisor has to find a replacement and then train them thoroughly in what they are to do. This takes time away from the other duties that HAVE to be done each day.

You know that new employee will probably be a bit slow to start so there goes the hours budget for a while. Now you have to answer for why you are over budget in that area.

While the new employee is "getting up to speed" you also run the risk of quality suffering which then can cause the customer to complain which then requires the effective supervisor to visit the customer and be an "ambassador" for the company and not make excuses. More time spent.

Then there are cases, depending on the circumstances, where an attorney may be involved in the issue. If that occurs, guess what? The supervisor spends more time away from the job talking with legal representatives. More time spent.

Do you see the many facets of an on the job injury--all of them taking time away from the job of satisfying the customer and producing quality work within the budget framework?

Wouldn't it just be a lot simpler if the effective supervisor makes a concerted effort AT ALL TIMES to assure that safety is a number one priority in their area?

Now let's address safety from the standpoint of,

"COMPANY FINANCES"

The company pays an insurance premium every year based on the payroll of the organization. It is generally a percentage of that payroll and is adjusted based on the safety record of the company. Let's look at an example of a safe company versus one that is in category 1. Let's assume the company has a $1 million dollar annual payroll and the state they operate in has a standard workers compensation rate of 3%. So this company, at regular published rates, would pay a premium of $30,000.

Companies are assigned what is call a "modification factor" depending on their history of safety. This rate changes each year but it is important to mention that whenever a major injury related accident occurs, that accident stays with the company rating for at least 3 years.

Now let's look at two companies with that $1 million payroll.

The first company has not paid much attention to safety and has a worker's compensation "mod" factor of 1.99. With 1.00 being the standard, it means that this company pays almost double premiums this year. The standard $30,000 premium for them goes up to $59,700 for the year.

Now let's look at company 2 which has addressed safety very seriously and is concerned for the well being of their employees. They have been able to reduce their "mod" factor to .55 so the standard premium of $30,000 referred to earlier, becomes $16,500 for this company. What a difference.

Let's take the whole thing another step. How does this difference in insurance premium affect the sales department's ability to compete on pricing as they present proposals to prospective customers? They are at a cost disadvantage on every presentation they make.

Let me provide a real life situation that occurred a few years ago that I am very familiar with. I discussed it in an earlier lesson but it is important and bears repeating. Remember the lesson repeating 6 times? This will be two on this one and I won't be repeating it 4 more times in this book.

A Building Service Contractor who had been servicing a large customer for over 10 years was disqualified from renewing the agreement for an additional 3 years, why? The customer was very safety conscious and had a hard and fast rule that they would not do business with any firm that had a "mod" factor greater than 1.00.

The incumbent contractor in this example had just reached 1.01 for the upcoming year and it disqualified them from continuing. They pleaded their case but to no avail. The customer's position was that if they made one exception they would end up having to make other exceptions and they were not going to get into that situation. I should also mention this was a large manufacturing facility and this segment of business is very conscious of injuries on the job and the possible repercussions. Remember reading about this is an earlier lesson?

There is always negotiations that take place on insurance but this example provides you a clear picture of what can happen to the company finances if safety is deemed not important in an organization.

Hopefully this lesson has brought to the forefront the importance of safety in the workplace and how it can and does affect the employee, supervisor, and the company's finances and ability to sell additional work. It ends up being a domino effect.

As you complete this lesson, here are some questions to answer.

1. How has an injury of a worker or workers affected my ability to be an effective supervisor?

2. What can we do to improve the safety in our company?

3. What role can I play to improve safety?

4. What is our worker's compensation rate and what can I do to help bring it down?

5. Our next step in safety will be_____?

6. Is every facility in my area operating as safely as it can? If not, why not and what will I do about it?

TWELVE LESSONS

NOW WHAT HAPPENS?

After weaving your way through 12 lessons on becoming an effective supervisor, interjecting your company's policies and procedures along the way, you should now have many of the tools needed to be a more effective supervisor. That is certainly our hope for you.

But what happens now? Are you going to say "that's nice" or are you going to take the information learned and apply it in your everyday work environment? The choice is yours.

If you thoroughly studied each lesson you should have become aware that the job of an effective supervisor is an important one as well as a demanding one. Take the information learned and use it to make yourself a more valuable asset to your organization AND to the employees you are responsible for supervising. You all win if you do that.

You have the satisfaction of furthering your career, the employees become more effective in what their role is, and your company becomes a more stable organization in satisfying the customer and adding more customers thereby enhancing your opportunity for growth and advancement.

Let me encourage you to keep a copy of this handbook close by, refer to it as often as needed, and use it as a training tool in developing employees that want to become supervisors. You all benefit from it.

We wish you the very best in your positive endeavors.

OTHER RESOURCES AVAILABLE FROM CONSULTANTS IN CLEANING, LLC.

BOOKS BY RICHARD OLLK, CBSE, RGC

SELLING CONTRACT CLEANING SERVICES 101

FINDING, TRAINING AND KEEPING GREAT SERVICE EMPLOYEES 101

THE DO'S AND DON'TS OF CONTRACT CLEANING FROM ONE WHO DID AND DIDN'T

TRAINING DVDS/CDS

DEALING WITH CULTURAL AND GENERATIONAL DIFFERENCES IN THE WORKPLACE

FINDING AND KEEPING GREAT HOURLY EMPLOYEES

TECHNOLOGY IN TRAINING

INCREASING PROFITS WITHOUT INCREASING SALES

CUSTOMER RELATIONS FOR SUPERVISORS AND CLEANING TECHS
(ALSO AVAILABLE IN SPANISH)

Richard D. Ollek, CBSE, RGC

BSC SUPERVISOR TRAINING

MAKING YOUR TRAINING MORE EFFECTIVE

DISCIPLINE TRAINING (ALSO AVAILABLE IN SPANISH)

WHY CAN'T THEY DO IT RIGHT?

GETTING THE NEW ACCOUNT STARTUP RIGHT

CONDUCTING AN EFFECTIVE BUILDING WALK THROUGH

KEY POINTS TO INCLUDE IN A CUSTOMER SERVICE AGEEMENT

SELLING STRONG IN TODAY'S ECONOMY

PROSPECTS YOU SHOULD NOT PURSUE

WHY SHOULD ANYONE BUY FROM YOU?

THE COMPONENTS OF A SUCCESSFUL SALES PROPOSAL

CLOSING THE SALE

All of these resources are available at www.consultantsincleaning.com. We continue to add new training materials on a regular basis so check back often to see what new resources have been added.

In addition, we publish regular free blogs that can be accessed by going to the web site and clicking on the blog icon.

Weekly free podcasts are also available at www.Kleancast.com. There you can subscribe so you are alerted whenever one is posted.

RICHARD D. OLLEK

BIOGRAPHY

Richard (Dick) Ollek is a 50+year veteran of the Building Service Contracting industry. In 1963 he took a position as Administrative Manager of a Sanitary Supply and Contract Cleaning company in Wichita, Kansas.

After spending 9 years with that firm, he started his own company and served as President and CEO until he sold it in 2005. During those nearly 34 years he was able to build a successful organization that operated several branch offices in 7 states while keeping the headquarters in Wichita.

After selling his company he formed Consultants In Cleaning, LLC where he now serves as President and CEO. The company has expanded to where they now offer many services such as,

....Personal, on location consulting assistance to individual companies. Dick does all of the on site visitations himself.

....Telephone consultations with those firms wanting to develop and grow their companies in sales and profits using Dick's proven systems and processes.

....Training and educational DVDs for all aspects of a company including sales, human resources, operations, and administration. Most of the DVDs are prepared in such a way that they can be taught by a company representative or used as a video at a general training session.

They are all done in conversational style, most with exercises to better engage the audience.

....A FREE weekly blog that is posted on his web site at www. consultantsincleaning.com.

....A FREE weekly pod cast that covers a wide variety of subjects to assist the viewer/listener become better at their job as well as assisting them to improve their overall life. These pod casts are available at www. kleancast.com.

....On location 1 and 2 day training workshops for individual companies that are tailored to that company's needs.

....In addition to his book on Effective Supervision, Dick has authored 3 additional books entitled,

SELLING CONTRACT CLEANING SERVICES 101

FINDING, TRAINING, AND KEEPING GREAT SERVICE EMPLOYEES 101

THE DO'S AND DON'TS OF CONTRACT CLEANING FROM ONE WHO DID AND DIDN'T

Year after year, Dick continues to be one of the most highly rated speakers at various industry conventions, workshops, and seminars in addition to many return engagements to individual companies.

He is a Certified Building Service Executive and has served as President of the Building Service Contracting Association, International (BSCAI).

Dick has become known for his frequent use of Ollekisms when they are appropriate such as,

...If you say that's not my job, chances are the one you have won't be yours much longer either.

....If all the training you do in your company is send the new recruit out to work with an "experienced" worker to "learn the ropes", the new recruit may just learn the ropes that will hang them if you haven't followed up to be sure the experienced worker is doing it right.

....Need to fire someone? Take them to lunch and buy theirs to go.

....If you're not training your employees because you think they will leave anyway, think what will happen if they stay.

Dick lives with his wife Barbara and the Boston Terrier dog Caesar in central Missouri on the Lake of the Ozarks near Camdenton.

Printed in the United States
By Bookmasters